Shady Characters

Plant Vampires, Caterpillar Soup, Leprechaun Trees, and Other Hilarities of the Natural World

by

Paul Hetzler

As noted in the Acknowledgments, portions of this work have appeared previously in serial publications and are gathered here with the permission of those publications.

Disclaimer: While this work refers to medicinal and other uses of plants and other aspects of the natural world, no health claims are hereby asserted or recommended by the author or publisher. In all cases, readers should consult with their health care professional for medical counsel.

ISBN-13: 978-0998606095

ISBN-10: 099860609X

Printed in the United States of America

Submitted for deposit in the Library of Congress

First Edition

Lexingford Publishing LLC

Los Angeles   New York   New Orleans   Hong Kong

www.lexingfordpublishingllc.com

Dedication

For Marie-Line, *mon Coeur*.

For Raven and Heron, my beautiful teachers.

Acknowledgments

There are so many people who deserve credit for getting this to print. A huge appreciation to Arthur Bell, my publisher and editor, for his hard work, even as he relocated 2,800 miles away.

Heartfelt thanks to my ex-wife Beth for her longtime friendship; to my children Heron and Raven for the privilege of parenting them, and for helping me mature somewhat; to my parents Joe and Deirdre, sisters Brigid and Nuala, and brothers Kieran and Karl, for tolerating me all this time. And to the Stokoes, expert farmers who are patient with gangly sprouts.

To Joe Bruchac for years of mentoring and friendship, also Bill McKibben, and former teachers Cindy Savage and Curt Stager. Very kind of you to comment on this book. (Hope you don't mind I cut out all the bad stuff.)

To the strangers, friends, and colleagues who bugged me to get these essays in print; to former friends and partners whose teachings live on (sorry I pissed you guys off)—a real thank-you.

Merci mille fois to my wife Marie-Line Bourdy, for her incredible patience, her unwavering faith in the Divine, and for demanding authenticity of me. *Je f--g t'aime!*

And most importantly, gratitude to the compassionate Universe, our partner in co-creation.

Table of Contents

Introduction

Every time I make primordial soup, it tastes terrible. Maybe some element is missing.

Roughly four billion years ago in the original batch of soup—or possibly it was a stew or even a soufflé; that detail is a bit hazy—single-celled organisms first made an appearance. For the next 2.5 billion years that's apparently all there was. I'm pretty sure our planet got a little bored towards the end of that phase.

But once multicellular life did show up, it was restricted to water, and so it was another billion years before anything interesting slithered onto dry land. More recently, that is over the last 400 million years or so, the whole planetary creation process looks like it has been a lot more enjoyable than in those early times.

Take platypuses (or playpodes if you want the correct Greek pedantic plural, and an excuse to feel smug), for example. With all due respect to these amazing animals, just the sight of one can provoke mirth. You have to wonder if Mother Nature shopped at Ikea when creating the animals, and after they had all been assembled, there was a little pile of washers, bolts and animal parts left over on the workbench. It must have seemed a shame to waste them, and so with a little force, and probably a stapler, they fit together (more or less) to form an adorable, egg-laying muskrat-duck combo.

And the hilarity doesn't stop there. These docile-looking, essentially toothless creatures are venomous. It's like Beatrix Potter drawing Peter Rabbit with poison fangs. The male platypus has a pair of leg spurs that can deliver a cysteine-rich protein cocktail harsh enough to kill a dog, and to cause severe and long-lasting pain in humans. To be fair to the platypus, it is not aggressive in the least.

Perhaps evolution had interns doing the design work back in the day, because although the female platypus has a matched set of ovaries, only the left one works. Ever. This left-ovary issue puzzled me until I realized, of course—the beast was likely made from leftovers.

Old Ma Nature must have been in the mood for a visual gag when the pangolin, a golden-brown, armor-plated insectivore native to parts of Africa and Asia, was invented. It's like she got an aardvark to mate with a globe artichoke. The pangolin is a scaly, thick-tailed creature with a defensive skunk-like spray and the ability to ball itself up like a pill-bug when threatened. While it resembles armadillos and anteaters, not to mention dragons, DNA testing indicates it may be more closely related to cats. If the dragon genome ever gets mapped I'm sure it will prove to be related to them as well.

Marine life, of course, is deeply bizarre, as the planet got a billion-year head start experimenting with making slimy stuff. Really, I find it remarkable that people actually swim in the sea. Why Mother Nature stocked the oceans with nightmares like glow-in-the-dark anglerfish and vampire squid is beyond me. And those are the benign ones. She has cone snails which deliver a tiny sting you don't feel until a few days later, just before you die. Deadly box jellyfish, lethal stonefish, Portuguese man-o-war—if you ask me, the surf is kind of a La Brea Tar Pit for drunk college kids on break and old guys in Speedos. Which in the latter case may be an acceptable loss.

There is a sea worm called *Eunice aphroditois* which owns

10

lightning reflexes, and razor-sharp scissors for jaws. And it's big—a recently discovered specimen in Japan measured nearly ten feet long. Affectionately dubbed the Bobbitt worm, this lovely is capable of slicing corals and fish clean in half. For larger prey, animals many times its size on occasion, it injects a powerful toxin that can reportedly numb a human permanently. How that is known, I haven't a clue, although I have certainly met people who appeared so afflicted.

Octopuses, or octopodes if you like, are the envy of Cirque du Soleil with their ability to change shape, color and even texture at will, and to shed an arm-tip if it gets trapped in an elevator door or something. Their 1,600 suction cups are adapted to escape from aquariums, but also to smell, and according to National Geographic, to store memories. Recently these intelligent creatures were seen using tools, which is great news because now we know who to hire for putting up drywall and other home repairs. They're adept at building shelters out of shells right now, but they might get the hang of impact drivers and belt sanders if we give them the chance.

Hammering together weird life-forms for fun is one thing; messing around with their behavior is another. Consider the fact that human females have the strongest drive to start a family—that is, the highest estrogen levels—in their late twenties to early thirties, while males have the highest testosterone at seventeen or eighteen. At that age, guys have the emotional maturity of a turnip, at best. So how was this arrangement intended to work out for the continuation of our species? Maybe so-called "cougars" are part of the natural order. Honestly, though, I think it was just for yuks. Evolution can be tedious at times—even the forces of nature need a good laugh now and then.

Hey, does anyone have a decent recipe for primordial soup?

Chapter One

Got Nature?

Whether it's a cross-country ski outing, a day at the lake, or just lying on your back under a tree, it's relaxing to be outdoors. We all need a break from our daily grind now and then, and there is evidence that being near trees and waterways soothe us more than a day off spent indoors.

Animals deprived of a natural habitat become violent after a time, and begin to exhibit behaviors not characteristic of their species. Social bonds break down, illness increases. This is true for all animals, without exception.

OK, guess this animal: It's in the phylum Chordata, indicating it has a backbone, which rules out bugs and crawlies, not a big clue. Its class is Mammalia, meaning females of this species produce milk to nurse their young. It's in the order Primate, which does narrow it down a lot. Its family is Hominidae, its genus is Homo, and sapien is the species.

Trick question, of course—it's us. It is true that humans are set apart from other animals in significant ways, but from the perspective of science we are very much a species of animal. And as such, we are hard-wired to be immersed in the natural world.

According to Dr. Frances Kuo from the University of Illinois at Champaign-Urbana, people who live in landscapes that lack trees or other natural features suffer as a result. Residents of poorly planned or blighted urban areas will show patterns of psychological, social, and physical breakdown similar to those observed in captive animals deprived of a natural setting.

Among other findings, Dr. Kuo's research demonstrates that regardless of their social or economic status, elderly people feel better and live longer if their homes are near a park or other green space, and that college students do better on cognitive tests if their windows face natural settings. Her research also shows that children with ADHD show fewer symptoms after outdoor activities in lush environments.

Worldwide, people are drawn to nature, even if it's only a picture. In particular, we find the savannah, where humans first developed 200,000 years ago, very appealing. We gravitate toward similar landscapes such as parks, and model our yards in the same way. Through our DNA, as well as other genetic material called epigenes, we are inextricably linked to the natural world.

This hard-wiring has been clearly demonstrated through real-time PET brain imaging. The types of patterns we encounter in nature, whether in pine cones, nautilus shells, diatoms, snowflakes, tree branches, or sand dunes are called fractal patterns. Bird song and the sound of waves breaking are sonic examples of the same thing. Fractal patterns, it turns out, profoundly affect us, inducing brain waves associated with positive feelings.

A February 2014 article in the British news site guardian.com outlines how hospital patients in rooms with tree views have shorter stays and less need for pain medication compared to patients without such natural vistas. It goes on to say that after just an hour in a natural setting, memory performance and attention span improves twenty percent.

Apparently, nature makes us nicer. Researchers at the University of Rochester report that greater exposure to the natural world leads people to nurture close relationships, value community more, and to be more generous.

As an arborist, I've long cited research showing that planting trees in urban areas reduces crime substantially. Trees also increase property values between five and twenty percent, and incidentally, get people to spend more money. Whether it's plants at the mall or trees in the downtown shopping districts, it turns out that people shell out more greenbacks in green spaces.

Not only do we respond to nature, we haven't lost our ability to engage with it. A recent study proved that humans can track pretty well by scent. Those with sight impairments have been using echolocation for years now, but another recent finding is that with practice we can learn to echolocate nearly as well as bats.

When asked if humans need nature, Dr. Kuo replied "As a scientist I can't tell you. I'm not ready to say that, but as a mother who knows the scientific literature, I would say, yes." Whether we need it or just want it, we are at our best in nature, so let's make sure that we and our children take every chance we get to reap its many benefits.

Chapter Two

Trees

All my friends are shady characters, many of whom are trees. Although I am a lapsed Certified Arborist (not to be confused with a fallen arborist, which is more painful), I am still obsessed and infatuated with trees.

Leprechaun Trees

An early memory of St. Patrick's Day is how angry it made my mother, who holds dual Irish-American citizenship and strongly identifies with her Celtic roots. It was not the day itself which got her Irish up, so to speak, but rather the way it was depicted in popular American culture: Green-beer drink specials at the bars and St. Patrick's Day sales in every store, all touted by grinning, green-clad, marginally sober leprechauns.

Although Mom stuck to the facts about Ireland; its poets, playwrights, and history, my aunts and uncles would sometimes regale us kids with stories of the fairy-folk, including leprechauns. These guys gave me nightmares.

According to my relatives, you did not want these little guys endorsing your breakfast cereal. They might look cute, but if you pissed them off—which reportedly was not hard to do—they were likely to kidnap or cripple you, steal your baby out of the crib, or worse. And one of the surest ways to incur their wrath was to cut down their favorite tree, the hawthorn.

Native to Europe and northern Asia as well as to North America, hawthorn is a slow-growing, short-maturing (20-25') tree with prodigious thorns which are strong enough to puncture tractor tires. Experts disagree on the number of species (hawthorns, not tires) worldwide; estimates range from hundreds to thousands. To be on the safe side, many references simply designate all hawthorns as *Crataegus spp.* Since they cannot tolerate shade, they are often found in fencerows and pastures, where lucky specimens may survive for a century or more.

It is these large, older, solitary hawthorn trees which have often been associated with fairy-folk in Ireland, Scotland, Wales, England, and other parts of Western Europe having Celtic heritage. Even today in many places, local laws protect hawthorn trees from being razed for road work or other development, and it is not hard to find people who still feel it is bad luck to cut down such a tree.

Many cultures around the world have a long tradition of various "little people." Oftentimes each type will look after a certain habitat, or even a specific plant or animal species. None of Cornell's fact sheets on hawthorn mentions leprechauns or other little folk, so I do not know why the Celtic fairies were so touchy about this tree. Perhaps they liked its fruit, or felt safe among its thorns, but I suspect it is because hawthorn protected them against heart disease, thus allowing them to live the unnaturally long lives they were reputed to enjoy.

A member of the rose family, hawthorn is related to apples, juneberries, and raspberries, so it is not surprising that its fruit is edible. Hawthorn berries, sometimes called thorn apples, haws, or haw apples, vary from tree to tree in terms of palatability. Haws are good for making jelly—in fact I make some most every fall—and at times have been an important food source for native peoples and pioneers. Its wood is very hard, prized for tool handles, fence posts and firewood.

Hawthorn blooms in May, when pastures and meadows are festooned with the brilliant white flowers. These fragrant and attractive blossoms have a rich history, dating back possibly a thousand years, of medicinal use as cardiac tonic. Today, hawthorn flowers and leaves are dried, powdered, and made into capsules, and also packaged as tea.

As western culture supplanted, and in many cases obliterated, indigenous cultures, Native wisdom was often discounted and ridiculed. While this trend has not yet reversed, it has certainly slowed these days, as more and more "folk remedies" are proven by science to be effective. Ginkgo, St. John's wort, quinine and digitalis are just a few examples of traditional medicine vindicated through research.

While hawthorn hasn't yet been endorsed by the American Medical Association, studies have shown that it does have beneficial cardiac effects. An article in the July 2002 issue of the *Journal of Cardiovascular Nursing* stated that hawthorn "...consistently demonstrates its ability to improve exercise tolerance and symptoms of mild to moderate heart failure." Numerous other studies, including a large-scale 2008 meta-review of past hawthorn research, have come to similar conclusions.

You can plant your own hawthorn, which is sure to attract pollinators and birds, if not fairies. Some cultivars such as 'Paul's Scarlet' have pink petals, and others like 'Winter King' hold their fruit long into the winter. More importantly, a number of thornless varieties are available; 'Ohio Pioneer,' for example. A hawthorn will establish easily, and is tolerant of a wide range of

19

soil types and pH, as well as of road salt and compaction. Even if you do not ingest any of its flowers or leaves, watching songbirds nest in its branches and eat its fruit is likely to do your heart some good.

Fables can be tricky to interpret. In the same way that catastrophe befalling those who try to chase a leprechaun to the rainbow's end to steal his gold is a cautionary tale against get-rich-quick schemes, perhaps the warning against hawthorn removal is because its flowers are important to our health. On the other hand, maybe it is just to spare us from irate leprechauns and sharp thorns.

Only Bury Your Tree After It's Dead

In springtime, driving around on weekends makes me sad. Invariably I'll pass someone out in their yard, shovel in hand, maybe with their kids or spouse, and they have a cute little tree from the garden center on one side of them, and a wicked deep hole in the ground on the other. If I wasn't so shy, I'd stop and offer my condolences, because clearly they are having a funeral for the tree.

Here's an arborist joke: What do you call a three-foot deep planting hole for a tree? Its grave. Tree root systems are broad—two to three times the branch length, barring an impediment—and shallow. Ninety percent of tree roots are in the top ten inches of soil, and 98% are in the top eighteen inches. Tree roots are shallow because they like to breathe on a regular basis. I think we can all relate to that.

Soil pores allow roots to get oxygen, which ultimately comes from the soil surface. Oxygen levels drop with soil depth, eventually reaching zero at some point. In silt, clay or loam soils, that point is less than three feet down. To make matters worse, adding compost or manure to a deep planting hole ensures the roots will suffocate, because microbes that break down organic matter will use up all remaining oxygen.

Every tree comes with planting instructions, even if there is no tag. To read these directions, find the spot near the base where the trunk widens out and the roots begin. This is called the trunk flare, and is the depth gauge. The trunk flare should be just visible at the soil surface. With a very small specimen, especially a grafted tree, this can be tricky. Basically find the uppermost root and park it about an inch below the surface.

Not all trees planted too deeply die, but they all suffer a lot, and even in the best cases it will take them years to catch up with a similar tree planted correctly. In general, smaller trees fare better than larger ones. Sometimes a little tree can survive by sending out fibrous (adventitious) roots from its stem just below the soil surface. The larger the tree, the less able these scrawny new roots can support its large top.

There is an old saying, "dig a fifty-dollar hole for a five-dollar tree." It may need to be adjusted for inflation but the idea still has currency. The planting hole should be saucer-shaped and 2-3 times the diameter of the root system, but no deeper—ever. Otherwise the Planting Police will ticket you. Not really, but if an arborist happens along, they may scowl ominously at you.

Before backfilling, remove all burlap and twine. Wire cages on ball-and-burlap trees should be cut away once the tree is positioned in the hole. Container-grown tree root systems may have circling roots that must be teased out straight, or they will become girdling roots years later and choke the trunk.

Adding loads of organic matter to the backfill likely dates back to ancient times, when folks might grab an arborist, if one was handy, and throw them in the planting hole. Possibly in response to this, arborists now recommend little or no additional organic matter in many cases.

In very sandy or heavy clay soils, moderate (up to 30%) amounts of peat moss, compost or other amendments can be used in the backfill. Do not add sand to clay, though—that is how bricks are made, and most plants do not grow real well in bricks. Adding more organic matter than one-third by volume can cause a "teacup effect," and roots can suffocate. Fertilizer is stressful on new transplants, so wait at least a year on that. In healthy native soils, a tree may never need commercial fertilizer.

Water thoroughly as you backfill, and prod the soil with a stick or shovel handle to eliminate large air pockets. Unless the site is very windy it's best not to stake the tree—movement is needed for a strong trunk to develop. Two to four inches of mulch over the planting area (but not touching the trunk) will help conserve moisture and suppress weeds. It's almost impossible to over-water a new transplant, but it does happen. Throughout the first season, check the soil every few days to be sure it's moist but not waterlogged.

Have fun landscaping, but please wait until after your tree dies to inter it.

Basswood Best for Wooden Bass

Having received my first pocket knife at age eight, I wasted no time in launching my career as a famous sculptor. How hard could it be, I thought, and gathered a pile of two-by-four lumber scrap ends which to carve. Thinking I should warm up before producing a Remington-inspired bucking bronco, I set about to make a fish.

Fresh from a rigorous Sharp Object Safety Class ("Always cut away from yourself, son. OK, get lost."), I was careful with the

blade. However, that lumber was tough and knotty, and after a while my hand started bleeding. Thus I learned about blisters. As they healed, I lowered my sights from carving to whittling sticks into mere shavings for no good reason, a skill to which I remain well-suited.

It's no surprise I tried to carve a fish. I was familiar with perch and bullhead and bass. If only I'd been familiar with basswood, and the idea that there's a difference between softwood, which is wood produced by conifers, and soft wood. Dimensional lumber like two-by-fours comes from softwood, which is soft enough to drive a nail through without splitting, but may not readily yield to a blade.

Soft wood, on the other hand, often comes from deciduous "hardwood" species, and is too soft for use as structural lumber.

Poplars and willows are soft-wooded, but for carving, basswood is tops. Not only is the wood soft, it's also consistent across grain and resists checking, or cracking.

While it's an obscure claim to fame, basswood is one of the best materials for making fire by friction. This is not as mysterious or difficult as it sounds—with a little practice you can start a fire in a minute or two with a bow drill and a dry basswood spindle and fire board.

Equally obscure, but just as fun and probably more useful is the fact that basswood's inner bark is the strongest plant-based fiber in our region. The bark peels readily in spring and early summer. It's then soaked 3-5 days until the inner bark separates into thin flexible strips. These can be braided and/ or reverse-wrapped into rope and string. It's something you can do while chatting or watching a movie, much like knitting. I've made basswood ropes over a hundred feet long, and it never felt like work.

I haven't taken a stab—so to speak—at carving in some time. I love seeing the exquisite detail in many basswood carvings, such as the song birds wrought by the self-taught "Bird Lady of Pierrepont," Hazel Tyrell, in whose house I now live. If only some of her artistic ability, or at least inspiration, would rub off on me.

Test Your Tree IQ

It seems horribly unfair to include a test in a book that is supposed to be low on the pain index, possibly even enjoyable, but no one is watching, so I hope you'll at least take a peek at the quiz below. Or you can skip ahead to the next section.

1) What is an arborist?

a. What a resident of Ann Arbor, Michigan calls herself or himself.

b. A person who is knowledgeable about trees and tree care. Certified Arborists have passed a comprehensive exam and must take continuing education courses.

c. As opposed to a *your* borist.

2) When tree planting, what's the ideal amendment to mix with soil in the planting hole?

a. Wheaties or other vitamin-fortified breakfast cereals.

b. In most soils, nothing. Poor soils may be amended with up to 30% organic matter.

c. An arborist.

3) Tree topping is:

a. Extra-thick maple syrup lumberjacks prefer on their ice cream.

b. The wrong way to reduce a tree's height. It weakens the tree and makes it hazardous.

c. The way a beaver spreads pond slime on bark before eating it.

4) What is tree wound dressing?

a. Salad dressing derived from tree-wound exudate, a delicacy.

b. A compound once used to seal over tree wounds but which is no longer recommended because it may actually hasten decay.

c. Covering tree wounds with gauze and surgical tape.

5) What is drop-crotch pruning?

1. We don't want to discuss that kind of thing here.

2. The right way to reduce a tree's height; called crown reduction.

3. Modifying normal pants to conform to a certain fashion style.

6) The best material with which to fill a tree cavity is:

1. Cement, steel pipes and scrap metal—whatever is handy.

2. Nothing, but in some cases polyurethane foam may be used.

3. Dental amalgam.

7) How deep should trees be planted?

1. Are you kidding? The deeper the better!

2. So the root flare is just at ground level.

3. Depends how many arborists you throw in the planting hole.

8) The root system of a mature tree is shaped most like:

1. A carrot. Everyone knows trees have big taproots.

2. A plate. Roots extend twice the branch length, and 90% of them are in the top ten inches of soil.

3. A Volkswagen beetle.

9) What are tree guys?

a. The ones wearing hardhats and carrying chainsaws, duh.

b. Wires or cables to temporarily support new tree transplants.

c. You mean tree *persons*.

10) Define the term "underwire tree."

a. A weak sapling shored up by heavy-gauge wire under its bark.

b. Naturally short tree species chosen to plant under utility lines.

c. Fruit trees that bear exceptionally large, voluptuous fruit that need extra support.

Answer Key:

Questions 1-4: "b."

5-8: "2"

9-10 "b"

What Grows on Trees

The old saw, "money doesn't grow on trees" will remain valid unless bartering ever becomes the norm, in which case fruit and nut growers will be awash in tree-grown currency. Figuring exchange rates could be quite a headache, I imagine. Our eastern white pine isn't considered a crop-bearing tree and it certainly doesn't sprout cash, but it has borne priceless fruit all the same.

The tallest trees this side of the Rockies, white pines as tall as 230 feet were recorded by early loggers. The current US champion stands at 188 feet, and in the Adirondacks we have several old-growth white pines over 150 feet.

In terms of identification, white pine makes it easy. It's the only native pine out east that bears needles in bundles of five, one for each letter in 'white.' To be clear, the letters are not actually written on the needles. White pine produces long, tapered cones having resin-tipped scales, perfect for fire starting and for making wreaths and other holiday decorations (might want to keep those away from open flames).

White pine is renowned for its exceptionally wide and clear, light-colored lumber used for flooring, paneling and sheathing as well as for structural members. New England was built on white pine, and in some old homes, original pine floorboards of twenty or more inches wide can still be found. Impressive as its premium lumber is, white pine's most precious gift is invisible. And hopefully indivisible.

Between a thousand and twelve-hundred years ago here in the northeast, five indigenous nation-states decided they spent too much energy disputing borders and resources. With the help of a visionary leader, they devised a federal system of governance to resolve inter-state issues, leaving each nation-state otherwise autonomous.

White pine, with its five needles joined at the base, helped Inspire the new federal structure. It remains an apt symbol for this confederacy, the Iroquois, or Haudenosaunee as they call themselves. The tree was, and is, depicted with a bald eagle, five arrows clenched in its talons to symbolize strength in unity, perched at its top.

The Confederacy comprises fifty elected chiefs who sit in two legislative groups, with a single elected head of state. Historically, only women could vote. Women also had the sole power to impeach leaders not acting in the public's best interest, and could quash any legislation they deemed rash or short-sighted. Every chief was expected to be able to recite the Iroquois constitution from memory, a feat which is still practiced today on some reserves, and takes nine full days to complete.

Benjamin Franklin and James Monroe wrote extensively about the Iroquois confederacy, and Franklin in particular urged the thirteen colonies to adopt a similar union. When the Continental Congress met to draft the Constitution, Iroquois leaders attended, by invitation, for the duration as advisers.

Among the earliest Revolutionary flags was a series of Pine Tree Flags, and the white pine remains on Vermont's state flag. The eagle with a bundle of arrows clutched in its talons, a uniquely Haudenosaunee symbol, has adorned US currency from 1797 to present day. If our coins and dollar bills were bigger, no doubt you would see the white pine directly below it. I suppose in a metaphoric sense, our money did grow on a tree.

29

A Place to Hang Your Hat and (Law) Suit

Tree topping is a subject I can really get worked up about. It's unprofessional, unsightly, outrageous, unethical, dangerous, and I suspect it may lead to more frequent rainy weekends and male-pattern baldness. It's unthinkable, horrible, and did I mention, bad! That should be pretty clear—any questions? Oh, exactly what is tree topping? Hang on. Mmmph—there, that's better. Had to wipe the foam off my mouth.

Tree topping is the removal of limbs and or/ trunks to an arbitrary length, leaving stubs. Variably known as heading, hat-racking or tipping, it is denounced by the Tree Care Industry of America, The International Society of Arboriculture and other professional tree-care organizations.

Topping is not to be confused with pollarding, a practice dating to feudal times when peasants could be put to death for cutting down the king's trees, but were allowed to clip each year's twig extension back to a callus "ball" for use as fuel and fodder. Pollarding does not work on all species, and to be successful must be started when a tree is relatively young, and continued annually.

Back to topping. It shortens a tree, but doesn't alter the tree's DNA which instructs it to grow to its species potential. After the natural branch structure is destroyed by topping, new growth erupts from the bark. These shoots, called epicormic sprouts, will become major branches. Unfortunately, they are poorly attached to the parent wood.

Because the tree is in a hurry to re-gain its genetically mandated height, the new branches grow faster than usual. You know haste makes waste, and as a tree cranks out these replacement limbs, it forgets to add much lignin, stuff that makes wood stronger. So now we have branches weaker than the originals, badly hitched up to the trunk or major branch wood.

But that is not all—there are two more things. Thing One is decay, which sets in at each topping wound. Our flimsy new branches soon find themselves attached to a rotting stub. It may take thirty years or it may happen in fewer than five, but every topping cut grows a killer limb. Of the precious few certainties in life, three of

them are "death," "taxes," and "tree topping creates hazards."

Thing Two is the tree's budget. A hat-racked tree has to take money out of the bank, or starch out of storage, to replace leaf-bearing wood at a time when much of its bank account, the starch contained within woody tissues, has been stolen and run through a chipper.

Trees need reserves to make defensive chemicals that protect against pests and decay, to expand root systems, and produce each year's leaves. A topped tree is weaker and is far more vulnerable to decay, disease, and insects than it had been before its "treatment." If a short tree is desired, a short-maturing species should be planted.

The sound of backpedaling is an unpleasant noise, but there is a

31

practice called "crown-reduction pruning" which can slightly reduce the height of hardwood trees while maintaining their natural architecture. Crown reduction takes a good deal of training to do properly. It can only reduce a tree's height 20-25 percent, and has to be repeated every 3-5 years as deemed prudent by an experienced arborist.

Another practice, called "crown thinning," addresses fears about a tree blowing over. This is the judicious pruning of branches evenly throughout the canopy to reduce wind resistance. A maximum of 20% of live branches may be removed. Again, this takes a great deal more skill than topping.

The International Society of Arboriculture, a research and education association of tree care professionals, advises the public that a tree company which advertises topping should not be hired for any work. Period. Like, don't let them set foot on your property. A company willing to top trees is by definition less than professional, and less likely to understand other elements of tree care, including basic safety procedures.

Tree topping is acceptable, however, for all who enjoy forty-foot hat racks, and liability lawsuits.

Hikers, Hunters, Stinky Socks and Wild Raisins

Hunters, hikers and others who traipse through the autumn woods have probably all been accosted at one time or other by a pungent odor akin to a rank locker room or an overripe laundry basket. Oftentimes this happens in or near a wetland, and the smell is strongest when the sun first hits.

The culprit is one or more of the many native shrubs and small trees in the genus Viburnum such as wild raisin, arrowwood and nannyberry. These humble plants are found throughout in the Northeast in fencerows, old pastures, forest edges, and especially in wetlands. They provide essential cover and nesting habitat for songbirds, and in late summer they bear sweet berries that are relished by birds and outdoor enthusiasts alike.

When viburnum leaves break down they give off butyric acid, a noxious chemical that in its pure, lab-made form is listed by the EPA as a toxic substance. Its smell has been likened to rancid milk, stinky feet and extreme body odor. Aside from a few industrial uses, butyric acid is added to some carp-fishing bait and has been found in homemade stink bombs deployed by pranksters and activists. Incidentally, it's also an ingredient in rooting compounds used in the nursery trade to propagate woody plants, including viburnums. There may be some kind of tree karma there, I'm not sure.

Some viburnums, most notably highbush cranberry, even have butyric acid in their fruit. The fruit of highbush cranberry, which is not a true cranberry, is an acquired taste, to put it mildly. Why this otherwise amiable shrub adds such a chemical agent to its berries is a mystery.

Of all viburnums, I think the leaves of wild raisin (*V. cassinoides*) are the most pungent. It's easy to forgive its funk because it has the best fruit. From late August through the fall and sometimes into the winter, you can find sweet, dark purple raisin-esque fruits in wetlands and on the edges of ponds. Relative to the size of the fruit, the seed is

rather large, but its flavor and sweetness make up for it. Sometimes the stinky-sock odor is what has alerted me to the presence of wild raisin, and I've sniffed out some good fruit that way.

I think everyone who enjoys the outdoors should get acquainted with the wild raisin, which can provide a welcome snack on a cold day. Hunters and hikers have an added incentive: Wild raisin's butyric acid-laced leaves could come in handy as a cover story for actual stinky socks back at deer camp or inside a cramped tent.

Shady Business

Sometimes it's good to have a few burly associates for protection, because when the heat's on and you need to lie low for a while, you can always turn to those shady characters for relief—those big guys with solid builds that no one pushes around. Yeah, the trees. They're cool.

When the thermometer hits eighty Fahrenheit and keeps climbing, any shade is welcome. If you're lucky enough to have mature trees where you live, not only can you get a break from the sun, but the air temperature will be five to ten degrees cooler than out in the open; natural air conditioning.

Speaking of which, if you use an air conditioner, having shade trees on the south and west sides of your home will reduce your cooling costs by a minimum of twenty percent, and possibly as much as fifty percent. It's like sending away for an electric-bill rebate except you save the stamp. Deciduous trees are ideal because they shield your home in summer yet allow sunlight through in winter when you want it.

On those blistering summer days when you think it's too hot to work outside, you're not alone—trees share your outlook. Photosynthesis, that remarkable process that turns carbon dioxide and sunlight into sugar (thereby keeping trees alive) and oxygen (thereby helping keep us alive), does not work well above eighty-five degrees. All that solar energy going to waste! Incidentally, leaves can get too hot in full sun even when the air temperature is moderate—kind of like the way an asphalt roof gets scorching in the sun.

This is why a tree's inner canopy is essential. Far from being unlucky residents of a less-desirable neighborhood, leaves that are shaded, and thus cooled, by the upper canopy are key players in a tree's survival, as they're the only ones on the job when it's too hot for their upstairs neighbors to work. So it's best not to get overly enthusiastic with pruning. Trees don't want their inner canopy "cleaned out" to any great extent.

Hopefully you're drinking plenty of water in the summer heat. It might surprise you that trees can run short of water, especially in seasons like 2012 and 2016. While we tend to think tree roots dive deep in search of a cool drink, ninety-eight percent of tree roots are in the top eighteen inches of soil. A few maple trees are exceptions in that they have "sinker roots" which extend much deeper, and are able to access more water. It is still a mystery how this works, because other tree roots suffocate for lack of oxygen at such depths.

A brown, dead-looking lawn will recover from a severe water shortage in a matter of weeks, because grass has a mechanism to become dormant without suffering harm to its roots. Trees, however, may take two to three years to fully recover from a very dry summer. Drought stress weakens a tree, making it more vulnerable to diseases and insects. While many shady characters don't take well to a good soaking, your tree will appreciate a thorough weekly drench. Forget the lawn—water the trees!

Here's to healthy, hydrated summers for you and all your shady associates.

The Root of the Problem

April showers bring stuff like May flowers, a chorus of spring peepers and other frogs, and backhoes. Spring is construction season, which for arborists and trees is also root-damage season.

From a tree's perspective, root injury is the source of all evil. Well, nearly all of it, anyway—chainsaws and forest fires aren't so kind to trees, either. But regardless of the worrisome signs a tree may develop, whether early fall leaf color, tip dieback, slow growth, or even some diseases and insect infestations, the problem is below ground in the majority of cases.

Part of the issue stems from a flawed understanding of tree biology. There is a lot of tree-root apocrypha floating around the public consciousness. One myth—let's call it the Legend of the Big Taproot—maintains that trees make enormous deep taproots. While the story allows that a few

side roots may branch off, the key element is the Big Taproot.

It's true that trees such as oaks and walnuts have a significant taproot when they're young, but in maturity their root systems look like a pancake, not a carrot, the same as other tree species. Most of us have seen trees that have blown down, but that monster taproot has yet to be spotted. It's no coincidence that the flat root system one sees on a windthrown tree is referred to as a root *plate*.

Tree roots are surprisingly shallow, and they extend, barring an obstacle such as a road or building, two to three times the length of its branches. This is a tree's root zone—a broad, shallow, vulnerable mass of roots.

Sadly, the Big Taproot Legend has dreadful health implications. For trees, at least—who knows what it portends for our well-being. If we believe tree roots like it deep, we won't think twice about adding fill, or even paving some of the root zone.

What's wrong with that? To survive, roots need oxygen, which they get directly from soil pores. Even though they make oxygen when they photosynthesize, trees can't transport it through their vascular tissues that work so nicely for carrying water, sugars, and nutrients.

Soil compaction from vehicles or equipment within the root zone causes the same problems. In wet soil conditions, even excessive foot traffic and habitual Morris dancing can cause enough compaction to mash soil pores shut and exclude oxygen. In these cases, roots slowly suffocate, and the tree will eventually show symptoms of decline.

Excavating or trenching within a root zone severs some tree roots and usually compacts the rest. Sometimes root damage will kill a tree outright within a few years, but more commonly there will be a prolonged decline over five to ten years or more. Because of the time lag, secondary, opportunistic agents often get the blame.

As with relationships, where trees are concerned, the problem at hand is very often not the real issue. Imagine glancing out the window one day to see wood chips the size of baseballs raining down from your favorite white pine. You rush outside with your Kevlar umbrella and discover an infestation of Jig Sawflies, their carbide blades gleaming as they chew their way down the trunk. As they smirk at you atop the mound of pine chips, you search the Internet for an exterminator, knowing you'll miss sitting under the pine's yellow foliage.

Wait a minute! Yellow foliage? How long was it like that? Maybe there's something else going on here. Fortunately, jig sawflies do not exist (as far as I know), but leaves and needles look like dinner to a heck of a lot of insects. A strong, happy tree will be able to respond to insect feeding by manufacturing chemicals known to scientists as Bad-Tasting Stuff to repel them (bugs, not scientists usually). It will endure some loss due to insect feeding, but it will be able to keep the balance in its favor.

Let's think back on your white pine. Wasn't that the one that you worked so hard not to hit with the backhoe when the septic went in six years ago? Or was that the one the gas company trenched near ten years ago? It doesn't matter. Human activity compromised the root system, resulting in the demise of the tree years later. Sawflies or no, that pine was doomed.

By now you may be thinking, I could sure use another coffee, or, how do trees in those little concrete squares (tree pits) in the sidewalk survive? The difference is that they are put there as little tykes and never come to depend on a normal root system. They've adapted to available root space and in technical parlance are "unhappy." Mature trees which have their large root systems suddenly cut or damaged to the size of tree pits are termed "dead."

You can preserve trees in a construction site by cordoning off the root zone at least to the tree's drip line (branch length) with snow fence before the project begins. Keep in mind that even stockpiling material under trees causes root damage. If driving near trees is unavoidable, adding four to six inches of wood chips or gravel (two-inch or larger) to the traffic pathway will help.

If excavation within the root zone is necessary, cut roots cleanly, flush with the trench wall. If possible, lay wet burlap over the root ends until backfilling is done. If more than 50% of a tree's root system needs to be cut, it's best to remove the tree. Any significant root damage, including compaction, can lead to future instability of the tree.

To repair damage already done, act quickly—once symptoms show up years later it's too late. Hire a tree care company to loosen the soil with high-pressure water or air injection. Soil injections of beneficial microbes in a solution of dilute sugars and various natural compounds have been shown to be valuable. If this isn't in your budget, aerating on a 2-foot grid using a soil auger (1-2" diameter by 18-24" long) will help.

Don't create raised bed gardens around trees or otherwise add soil to the root zone, and try not to drive or park within it. So long as the soil isn't wet, Morris dancers are acceptable, but not on a regular basis, and only if they first remove their bells.

Got Gas?

Some foods give you gas, but early spring is the time of year when gas gives you a really delicious food. Maple syrup, which is nutritious enough to be listed by the USDA as a food (I say it deserves its own Food Group designation), is gas-powered. Carbon dioxide-powered, to be specific. If it wasn't for a bunch of little gas bubbles in the xylem tissue, maple sap would not flow. Who knew that wood was carbonated?

A mere dozen years in the past, science was at a loss to explain what caused maple sap to run. I always like it when people who are smarter and better-paid than I am don't have the answer, either. We always knew that below-freezing nights and warm days lead to sap flow. But it wasn't until recently that the mechanism behind it was understood.

Throughout sugar maple's range, maple production has been economically important since Native Americans first taught European settlers how to gather maple sap to make syrup and sugar. Back then it involved placing red-hot stones into containers of sap to boil it down. We're all thankful that technology has improved. Today's maple producers have reverse-osmosis units, vacuum pumps and efficient high-capacity evaporators.

Aside from maple, very few tree species have a spring sap run. Birch and butternut are exceptions, but their roots generate pressure that forces sap upward, which is not the case in maples. It turns out maple sap flow is due to the way its wood interacts with freeze-thaw cycles. In biology we learned that wood, or xylem, is responsible for upward transport of water and dissolved nutrients, while sugars move down through the phloem, the outermost layer of cells. Fortunately for us, xylem misbehaves during the spring sap run, ferrying sugars upward where we can get to them. Later in the season, xylem casually returns to the textbook model, acting as if nothing unusual happened.

Xylem is composed of several types of cells, including vessels to transport liquid, and fiber cells to provide strength. Unlike most trees, maples have fiber cells which are partially gas-filled. Carbon dioxide and other gases in those fibers are critical to generating flow because they dissolve in sap. The geyser that results when we open a seltzer bottle, especially a warm one, too fast is a reminder that plenty of carbon dioxide can dissolve in water. If that bottle is icy cold, the risk of a gusher is low because cold water holds more dissolved gas.

During the night, gases in fibers shrink as they cool, eventually dissolving into sap in the vessels. This contraction of gases causes the tree's internal pressure to drop, creating a suction that draws sap up from the roots. As the temperature warms in the morning, gases bubble out of solution and expand, increasing the tree's internal pressure and forcing sap out the tap hole at about 15 pounds per square inch (psi) on average, occasionally up to 40 psi.

Rather than flowing up from the roots and out the tap during the day as was once commonly thought, sap actually flows down from the crown (in addition to some lateral flow) toward the tap hole. When a warm day follows a sub-freezing night, sap may run for a few hours or up to several days, depending on the tree, and factors like barometric pressure changes. If temperatures remain warm at night or below freezing during the day, sap will not run.

Using vacuum changes this picture because it reduces a tree's internal pressure. A tap hooked up to vacuum will yield twice as much sap as one that isn't. Even a sapling will yield quite a bit sap if vacuum is applied to its severed trunk. Of course it will have a very short life—a tree needs a full complement of leaves to produce enough sugar to support itself.

All native maples yield sweet sap. Although sugar (hard) and black maples are most commonly used, producers will also tap silver and red maple if available. Even the much-maligned boxelder belongs to the genus *Acer* and can be tapped. And though I hesitate to admit it, the Norway maple, which along with its red-leaf cultivars is listed as an invasive species, can be used.

Maple sap is two to three percent sucrose on average, although sugar content can range from one up to ten or more percent. In addition to sugar, sap contains organic acids, amino acids, minerals and other compounds, many of which contribute to maple's flavor. During the boiling process, an insoluble sediment composed of sugar and calcium maleate forms. This is called niter or sugar sand, and is filtered out.

If tasting great is not incentive enough to use maple syrup, consider its health benefits. One 100-gram serving of maple syrup provides more than 100% of the recommended daily amount of manganese and vitamin B-2, and is a significant source of magnesium, zinc and calcium. In 2016, a Toronto-based research team announced they had identified a compound in maple syrup that may inhibit beta-amyloid brain proteins from clumping, which could help prevent Alzheimer's disease.

The freeze-thaw, dissolved-gas, pressure-differential explanation of sap flow has some holes, though. While the mechanism should work with pure water, it turns out that sap only flows if it has a minimum level of sucrose. Flow should also happen in all xylem tissue, not just the living sapwood, but that's not the case either. So the mystery of sap flow continues. Sometimes it's a relief not to have all the answers.

Recently, a higher percentage of maple producers have been

branching out, you might say, into value-added products like maple cream and candy. Another item gaining in popularity is maple sap. Fresh sap is filtered, pasteurized, bottled, and then— carbonated of course. What goes around, comes around, it seems.

Nerd Holidays

Muskrat Day. Velcro Appreciation Month. Hair Follicle Hygiene Week. Arbor Day. You know it's an obscure event when the greeting-card trade hasn't bothered to capitalize on it. I like to think that the industry realizes Arbor Day is worthy of a Hallmark line, but that they have chosen to honor its spirit by conserving paper. C'mon, it's possible.

While it may not be the best-known observance, Arbor Day has a respectable history. Begun in 1872 by Adams, NY native J. Sterling Morton, Arbor Day was intended to highlight the need to conserve topsoil and increase timber availability in his adopted state of Nebraska. Though it began as an American tradition, Arbor Day, which is observed on the last Friday in April, is now celebrated in many countries.

Not only was Morton passionate about planting trees, for him the act was sacred. He said "The cultivation of trees is the

44

cultivation of the good, the beautiful and the ennobling in mankind," and believed that every tree planted made this nation a little better. Julius Sterling's son went on to fame with the Morton Salt Company, and Arbor Day went on to become an obscure, if virtuous, tradition.

I tend to agree with Morton's lofty pronouncement. To plant a tree is to invest in the future, and it is an act of generosity and of responsibility. When we add a tree to our community, it's likely that many generations of people will enjoy it long after we are gone.

Trees add value to our lives in surprising ways. Some of us have heard the spiel about the way trees decrease home energy costs, increase property values, filter pollutants and all that. But I'll bet few of us realize that green attracts green. Shoppers spend more money when there are trees in a downtown shopping district, and homes sell faster on tree-lined streets.

Hospital patients who are able to view trees from their beds have better health outcomes. Studies have shown that crime rates drop significantly when trees are planted in urban neighborhoods. And it may come as a surprise that lying under a tree in summer cures acne. OK, I made that up, but the rest is true.

Although it is noble to plant a tree, it has to be done right or you may as well rent it—a poorly planted tree will only live a fraction of its potential lifespan. Location is the first consideration. Kids and trees generally look cute when you bring them home from the nursery, but they grow up fast and often take up more room than expected. If your site is under utility lines or has restricted space for branches or roots you need the right species and variety that can grow to full size without causing conflicts.

Because ninety percent of tree roots are in the top ten inches of soil, the planting hole should be saucer-shaped and two to three times the diameter of the root system, but no deeper. It's imperative the root flare be right at ground level, because deep planting leads to serious health problems. For the tree, primarily.

Before backfilling, remove all twine, which will choke the tree, and burlap, which will encourage girdling roots and delay establishment of a normal root system. Wire cages on ball-and-burlap trees should be cut away. Container-grown trees may have circling roots that need to be cut and teased out straight.

Fertilizer is stressful on new transplants, so wait at least a year before adding any, and even then, only do so if a soil test indicates it is required.

Water thoroughly as you backfill, and prod the soil to eliminate large air pockets that can dry out roots. Unless the site is very windy it's best not to stake. Much like we exercise to increase strength, trees have to experience movement for strong trunk development. Spread two to four inches of mulch over the planting area to help conserve moisture and suppress weeds, but pull mulch a few inches away from the trunk. Throughout the first season, check the soil every few days to be sure it's moist but not waterlogged.

If you're looking for suggestions, here are some bullet-proof trees for street and yard planting:

Hawthorns are small, disease-resistant trees with copious white flowers in spring and bright red fruit which hang on through the winter to feed birds. It also tolerates road salt. 'Washington' and 'Winter King' are excellent cultivars.

The Japanese tree lilac is another small tree suitable for planting under utility lines. It is tough and drought-tolerant, and bears large cream-colored flowers. 'Ivory Snow' is a popular choice.

River birches are medium-large trees with pinkish-white exfoliating bark, and have few pest and disease issues. 'Heritage' is a proven cultivar.

Honeylocusts are also medium-large, and will tolerate wet soils, drought & road salt. Choose a thornless cultivar such as 'Skyline.'

The hackberry is a tall, drought-tolerant tree whose tiny berries are enjoyed by birds. Over time its bark becomes deeply grooved, bringing unusual texture to the landscape. 'Prairie Pride' is a good choice.

Kentucky coffeetrees are tall, drought-tolerant, and free of pests and diseases. Very coarse-branched, they add interest in winter.

Bur oaks get extremely large, and can live hundreds of years, sometimes 800 or more. They withstand all sorts of harsh conditions such as drought and intermittent flooding.

Have a happy Arbor Day this April—planting a tree is a wonderful activity to share with loved ones, and a great investment in the future.

Marshmallow Trees

I don't know about you, but I really look forward to those sticky evenings around a campfire. Not the sweltering kind of sticky, mind you. I'm thinking of the smoke-dodging, s'more-making nights spent with family and friends, wishing for fewer mosquitoes and more wet-wipes. Proper marshmallow toasting requires a high tolerance for concentrated sugars, plus a good stick. Marshmallows and a fire are helpful, too.

Someone once asked what kind of tree yields the best marshmallow stick. It seemed obvious since the process for locating the right stick historically involved two criteria: It must be 1) close at hand, and 2) long enough to avoid burning oneself. However, it occurred to me if it's a fresh-cut live branch, the species of tree is important.

Wild (black) cherry has tasty pea-size fruit, but its inner bark and leaves contain cyanogenic glycosides that are converted to cyanide in the body. These compounds are destroyed when heated to the boiling point, which is why livestock have been poisoned from consuming black cherry leaves and twigs: they neglected to cook them. Although the amount of cyanogenic glycosides in the tip of a black cherry branch is probably tiny, it's something to consider.

Yellow and black birch trees produce methyl salicylate, or wintergreen oil. Not only is a birch branch safe to use, it's delicious. Birch twigs were once the source of commercial candy flavoring, so you'll get a marshmallow with a slight wintergreen zest. Then afterward you can cut a fresh birch twig and chew the end a bit to make yourself a traditional camp toothbrush, minty flavor included.

Willow branches contain salicin, which our bodies convert to acetylsalicylic acid, or aspirin. Willow has been used for pain relief for thousands of years. Our native black willows, the ones that grow very large on stream banks, have the highest salicin content of any willow. Cut a black willow stick, take two marshmallows, and call me in the morning.

Witch hazel bark is an effective astringent, which means it constricts body tissues. Its leaves and bark are still used to make various over-the-counter products to relieve eczema, hemorrhoids and other ailments. Using this type of branch is perfectly harmless, but unless you need help puckering up, don't eat the witch hazel marshmallows.

Many of our native viburnums such as wild raisin and arrowwood give off volatile chemicals called butyrates after they're cut, compounds which smell akin to dirty socks. I don't know how long it takes a fresh-cut viburnum branch to smell rank. Feel free to experiment, preferably downwind from your friends.

Buckthorn is an invasive understory tree with glossy leaves and dark purple to black berries. As its name implies, it has thorn-like twig spurs, so you're not likely to choose a buckthorn branch in the first place. But they grow just about everywhere, so watch out. They're not deadly but their species name is *cathartica*, which gives you a clue as to their effects. A buckthorn marshmallow could leave you guarding the outhouse all night.

Our native hawthorn, on the other hand, is OK to use. An ambitious and very cautious camper probably could impale and roast half a dozen marshmallows on the long slender thorns of a single hawthorn branch.

The resin in pine, spruce and cedar branches is nontoxic, but they're seldom used for roasting. No sense getting sticky before the marshmallows go on, right? Dogwood, ash, maple and elm make good marshmallow sticks, safe but without any smells or whistles. But then maybe given some of the choices you'll want to stick with boring.

Ade for What Ails You

One of the brightest—almost electrified—fall leaf colors hails from a humble source. Farmers may consider the ubiquitous sumac a weed, and folks mistakenly believe it's dangerous. Its reputation as a nuisance stems from its habit of creeping into fields and pastures by means of its root system, but our native staghorn sumac (*Rhus typhinia*) is in no way a hazard. And its vibrant red-orange leaves that seem to wave to us from highway and byway in autumn are almost unparalleled in their brilliance.

Just as Dorothy learned there were good witches and bad witches in Oz, I had to learn about good and bad sumac. When I

was a kid, Dad showed me poison ivy and also warned, sight unseen, against poison sumac. Much the way "Marco" always went with "Polo," "poison" was followed by either "ivy" or "sumac" in my mind. I was an adult before discovering the truth. Staghorn sumac is not only safe to touch, its fruit tastes great.

Mind you, poison sumac is real. It's just that few people ever see it. If you do, as I have, you'll be ankle-deep in water. Poison sumac grows in swamps, and other than the fact it has compound leaves and is a shrub, it is really not all that similar to the sumac we see every day.

Poison sumac has loose bunches of berries that turn from green to off-white as they mature, and the clusters droop down. It has smooth twigs, and glossy leaves that turn yellow in the fall. "Good" sumac, on the other hand, bears red berries in tight cone-shaped bunches, proudly held up like Lady Liberty's torch. Staghorn sumac also has fuzzy twigs, and matte-finish leaves which become red in autumn.

The substance that makes apples tangy is malic acid, and sumac berries are loaded with this tasty water-soluble flavoring. To make "sumac-ade" all you need is a clean plastic bucket full of sumac berry bunches—don't bother picking berries individually. Fill the bucket with cold water, agitate the berries for a few minutes and strain through a clean cloth. This leaves you with a very sour pink beverage akin to dilute lemon juice. Sweeten your sumac-ade to taste, and serve with ice.

Because malic acid is water soluble, sumac berries lose some (but by no means all) of their flavor due to rains, which leach it out. But even in the spring you'd be surprised how tangy the berries can be. They are also a food source for American robins and other migratory songbirds in those years when their travel agents mess up and the birds arrive before the snow is gone. I have no idea if they care about the flavor, though.

There are other species of good sumac in addition to staghorn, and they all produce the same red berry clusters that aim heavenward. Some people actually plant sumac in the landscape both for the fall color and to attract birds. I know of at least two staghorn sumac cultivars; these and additional species such as oak-leaf sumac are available through specialty nurseries.

The next time sumac's bright autumn flag catches your eye, consider stopping to collect some berries to make a refreshing beverage.

Helicopters and Handkerchiefs: Signs of Stress

After the severe and unprecedented droughts of 2012 and 2016, the following years were characterized by spring pollen storms, and in a related development, a rain of helicopters in summer. It had nothing to do with aircraft, and everything to do with stress.

Short-term, moderate pressure—for example an article deadline—can be a positive force because it pushes one to act. However, we all know about the effects of undue stress: weight gain, increased risk of stroke and heart attack, difficulty concentrating, and more. We also know that other animals respond to stress negatively.

But if you have ever wondered what stress does to trees, well, you're in the minority, that's for sure. In a year following a drought, we all experience the results of tree stress in the form of high pollen loads. Most trees are wind-pollinated, which means their flowers are drab, because they merely have to attract the wind, which is way easier than attracting bees, something that requires nectar and bright colors. It also means their pollen is light, and travels far and wide. Even though it is barely noticeable, many willows, elms, maples, and poplars are in flower even before the snowbanks melt, and unless it is an unusually rainy spring, we would end up breathing a lot more tree pollen than in most years.

Obviously, trees do their reproductive thing on a regular basis, or they wouldn't still be here. Trees like willow and poplar flower every year. Others such as maple, oak and beech may produce few if any flowers for one or more years, followed by a "mast year" in which they bear a heavy seed crop. While mast years may occur once every two to seven years, 2013 and 2017 were much more uncommon situations.

In those years, many hardwoods pushed out flowers far in excess of any mast year. Heavy seed production following severe stress, known as a distress crop, is well-documented in Western forest stands under significant threat by pests, diseases or drought. It appears to be a bid to keep the species going at the expense of the current generation of trees. Sugar maples in particular bore a distress crop, something not seen before in the Northeastern US.

It is in the middle of the growing season that trees "choose," based on how much energy they have squirreled away in the form of stored starch, how many flower buds will bloom the following year. In other words, the relative abundance of flower buds reflects the conditions of the previous summer. This makes perfect sense: a tree makes only as many seeds as its energy budget will allow. During a year with plenty of moisture and sun, it will set loads of flower buds, and in a dry year, not so many.

There is an exception to this pattern, however. A distress crop is different in that the accounting department is left out of the loop. If conditions are stressful to the point that a tree's very survival is threatened, it gets triggered to release stored food reserves to make an ultra-heavy seed crop, even if it needs those reserves to survive the next year.

Forester Michael Snyder, former Commissioner of the Vermont Department of Forests, Parks and Recreation, explained it further in a *Northern Woodlands* magazine article:

> "...trees need to produce seed to pass along their genes and perpetuate their kind. It is so important that...they

react to impending doom by shifting their precious and hard-won resources away from their own growth and focus on the next generation."

The first recorded instance of a Northeast hardwood distress crop was in 2013, following the unprecedented (in terms of low soil moisture) drought of 2012. Sadly, 2016 was even worse, with soil moisture at record lows in many parts of the US. On sites with

thin soils, the effect was that much more severe. Affected trees are under tremendous stress, and will be more vulnerable to secondary agents such as pathogens and insects.

For several reasons, maple seeds are of particular interest. I guess it is their aerodynamics that grab my attention. Known to botany geeks as samaras, maple seeds have a broad wing that makes them spin, helicopter-like, as they fall, prolonging their flight and allowing them to travel some distance. In most cases it's a one-way flight, although many children, mine included, go through a phase where they'll scoop handfuls of these winged seeds—along with the requisite amount of dirt—and fling them aloft, delighted with their helicopters. But maybe there's an app for that now.

In addition to the imported Norway maple, we have four native species of large maples—sugar, red, silver, and boxelder

54

(surprise, that's a maple)—and several understory maples as well. All of these produce helicopter seeds. One of the side effects of tree seeds is a boom of baby trees. The spring of 2014 was fun as the distress-crop maple seeds germinated and Lilliputian maple forests carpeted lawns and gardens.

Whether it is a normal, heavy, or distress crop of maple seeds next season, I hope you get a chance to get out in the non-virtual world and get a few helicopters in your hair.

Freeze-Pops: Exploding Myths and Trees

When the temperature dips well below zero Fahrenheit, especially if it falls precipitously, things pop. If you are my age or older, that may include knees or other joints. Wood siding creaks. Frozen lakes and ponds emit ominous groans, snaps and booms that reverberate through the ice. And if soil moisture is high and frost quite deep, even the earth can shift in a harmless localized *cryoseism*, or "frost quake" that produces a nerve-rattling bang.

Those who spent time in wooded areas during northern winters have probably heard trees popping and cracking during a deep freeze. It's an eerie sound on an otherwise still night. Native peoples from northern regions were very familiar with this sound, and some even named one of the winter months in honor of it. The Lakota call February *cannapopa wi*, "moon when trees crack from the cold." The Arapaho consider December the tree-cracking time; for the Abenaki, it's January.

I once found a reference in a novel to exploding trees. In the book, a lost boy survives a northern winter so cold that some trees explode into smithereens. I had lived through winters with minus-40F temperatures but had neither seen nor heard of exploded trees. What did this author know that I didn't?

After much research, I discovered this: fiction is sometimes, well, fictional. Just as I thought, trees don't blast themselves to bits. But since that first reference I've encountered the exploding-tree myth a number of times. So what does happen when trees go 'pop' in the night (or day)?

As we all know, when water freezes, it expands. Luckily, sap is not pure water. It's endowed with antifreeze in the form of sugars, and to a small extent, dissolved minerals.

The more sugar or solute of any kind that is mixed with water, the lower the freezing point becomes. This is due to something known as the "Colligative Property of Solutions," as you may recall from General Chemistry. There comes a time, however, when even sugar-fortified sap will freeze and expand. This may rupture the bark of a tree, resulting in an audible crack as well as a visible one. In most cases frost cracks close with no long-term

56

ill effects, but sometimes they will become perennial.

Since it's a weak point, an old frost crack will easily re-open in cold spells. Then each spring and summer the tree will make callus tissue in an attempt to grow over the injury, resulting in a raised lip along the seam. Such trees have reduced timber value and an increased potential for decay to set in.

There's nothing one can do for frost-cracked forest trees in terms of prevention or treatment. You can protect young landscape and fruit trees, though, with light-colored trunk wraps, or even a coat of interior-grade white paint, on the lower trunks. Promptly remove wraps in the spring before they become havens for insect pests. Also, cracks or wounds should never be coated—this well-intentioned gesture can actually hasten decay.

In truth, trees do explode occasionally—if you place dynamite in them. A friend of mine contracted with the US Forest Service in the Northwest in the 1980s to create habitat for cavity-nesting birds. He climbed large spruces and firs, drilled a hole in the trunk halfway up and inserted a charge, which was later detonated from a safe distance. I'm pretty sure he preferred to do this "tree-popping" work when it was not below zero.

Wrapping Up the Northern Gum Crop

Recently I heard that gum trees abound in northern New York State, even at high elevations. I couldn't believe it until the person making this claim produced a pack of gum that was "made from northern hardwoods," according to its label. There it was in writing, and they wouldn't print it if it wasn't true, right?

I had tried spruce gum, a wonderful substance which makes your mouth taste like turpentine and will pull out dental fillings if chewed for longer than three seconds. It's an acquired taste, they tell me.

And I knew that sour gum, *Nyssa sylvatica*, a tree known for its intensely red fall foliage, can be found as far north as the southern Adirondacks. Sweet gum, *Liquidambar styraciflua*, (now there's a creative alias) is even less hardy and grows in balmier climes (i.e., south of Albany). But neither of these northern hardwoods is used to make gum.

Further inspection of the label revealed it wasn't the gum that was made from birch trees, it was the sweetener it contained, xylitol. The word xylitol is derived from the same Greek root as

xylem, which is what everyone except science geeks calls "wood." So it's not a surprise this naturally-occurring sweetener is found in birch sap. It may seem odd, though, that it's also in beets and even the human body, which makes about 15 grams of it a day.

Turns out that Xylitol is effective at cutting the frequency of childhood ear infections, and possibly in reducing the severity or duration of same. Research suggests that gum is better than xylitol-based candy in this regard.

And it may improve oral health. The Journal of the American Dental Association recently cited a study that found "Xylitol is an effective preventive agent against dental caries." Six to seven grams of xylitol per day is reportedly an ideal quantity for cavity prevention.

Because it has a low glycemic index, a scale that ranks carbs on how fast the body converts them to glucose, of 7 (compared to 68 for sugar), xylitol is safe for diabetics. Plus, it has one-third fewer calories than sugar. Wow, what's not to like about this birch-based miracle?

Well, except for a few small health-food companies, most commercial xylitol is made in an industrial lab. Xylan, a precursor compound found in hardwood fiber, corn cobs and various other plant material, is converted to xylose. This in turn is hydrogenated to form xylitol using a nickel-aluminum alloy. Someone probably checks for metals residue in commercial xylitol from overseas, on a regular basis. That's a safe assumption, I'm sure.

Xylitol can cause bloating and gas in some people. Oh, and it's extremely toxic to dogs. Well, nothing's perfect.

When the Wind Blows

When the wind blows, the cradle—presuming somebody left one in a tree—will rock. The arborist may or may not rock during a wind storm, but they will definitely be thinking about potential wind damage to trees. A critical factor that predisposes a tree to wind damage is weakness in major unions, also called forks or crotches. Failure of a large trunk-to-trunk union can be catastrophic, both for the tree as well as for people or structures beneath it. Luckily, most weak unions can be remedied once they're identified.

The dormant season is a good time to evaluate mature hardwoods for all kinds of defects, including weak unions. It's fortunate that unions provide clues as to their strength. The first is the angle of attachment. Unions close to ninety degrees tend to be strongest, while narrower ones are weaker. A tree with a narrow fork between two ("codominant") trunks that lean out away from each other is more at risk of splitting than such a tree where its codominant trunks are upright.

The next clue is the presence of seams—look for cracks running down the trunk from the union. A crack on both sides of the trunk implies a far weaker situation than does a single seam. Decay is an important clue, but the problem is that it's not always evident. Conks (shelf fungi) and woodpecker activity indicate serious rot, and it should go without saying that having a little "garden" of brambles and saplings growing in the fork also means extensive decay.

One of the clearest signs of weakness is a pair of ears on a fork. I should probably explain. Trees are self-optimizing; that is, they respond to stress by adding tissue in ways appropriate to the problem. The weaker a union, the more a tree compensates by adding wood, in this case outward from the trunk in a sort of "ear" or "clam shell" shape.

Finding one of these clues is enough to warrant professional advice, and if you see more than one sign, make it soon. So long as a tree is in generally good condition, even the weakest union can usually be stabilized with a cable brace two-thirds to three-quarters the way to the top from the union. Because a mature shade tree is irreplaceable in one lifetime, and because it's a slight inconvenience to have a large portion of one "drop in" on you suddenly, cabling is worth it.

Every component in a cable system is load-rated, and sized differently for each situation. With all due respect to the capable "DIY" crowd out there, the wrong cable is worse than no cable. Cabling should only be done by someone familiar with the American National Standards Institute (ANSI) published standards for cable bracing. This is an important point; not all tree care professionals are up to snuff on ANSI standards.

Incidentally, the reason that cradle was rocking in a tree? In many Native cultures such as the Haudenosaunee (Iroquois), mothers would secure an infant's cradle board—the original baby backpack—to a tree while they tended crops or did other work. The child thus got a pleasant, shady, adult's-eye view of the world, and was always taken down if the wind became too brisk.

That Old Line on Why Leaves Change Color

Very few people remember that years ago we only had orange fall color, thanks to carotenoids in the leaves, but without yellows or reds, which are due to xanthophylls and anthocyanins, respectively. Then in the 1930s, the Hoover Administration rolled out new leaf-color enhancement legislation to boost tourism in the Northeast as a response to the Great Depression. It was called the Hoover Omnibus Anthocyanin and Xanthophyll bill, or HOAX.

OK, it's unlikely it happened that way, but hey, I wasn't alive then, so who knows? We know more about fall color today than when I was a kid, but we still don't understand it all.

As a wee lad I was told a story wherein the bright summer sun would bleach pigment from clothes hung on the line, and save up the colors to paint on autumn leaves. Thinking back on that yarn it occurs to me that solar dryers (a.k.a. laundry lines) and fall leaf color change are similar in how they operate. They're both elegant and cost-free, but their performance depends on the weather.

The same clear-sky conditions that produce dry, fresh-smelling (and just a teensy bit faded) laundry also make for the best leaf color. While the former process is well-understood, the latter is a story fraught with murder and intrigue, and requires some explanation.

Chlorophyll, the green molecule at the center of the photosynthesis miracle, is what makes the world go 'round. Some say money is, but those people need a reality, um, check. Without chlorophyll the sole life on Earth would be bacteria, whereas without money we'd merely have to adjust to a barter system. Given that chlorophyll and currency are both green, it's easy to understand the mistake.

Green gives way to fall colors, though, when trees start killing their own chlorophyll, revealing yellow xanthophylls and orange carotenenoids that were in the leaves all along. How could a tree be so heartless as to slay its chlorophyll? Aside from the obvious—it doesn't have a heart muscle—the answer is to keep from drying to a crisp in the winter.

Each leaf is jacked into the tree's circulatory system: water and nutrients enter, sugars exit. In autumn these connections have to be sealed or the open vascular tissue would allow moisture to seep out and pathogens to get in. When the days shorten to a certain point, trees start to make a waxy plug, or abscission layer, between leaf and twig, thus choking chlorophyll and rolling out the new color scheme.

Yellow and orange, as we learned in high-school Biology, are hidden under green, but whence comes red? This is where the mystery begins. We know that warm sunny days and cool nights result in more red color, and that relatively few tree species produce red fall color.

In case anyone asks you, which I realize is unlikely, you can tell them the chemicals responsible for the red and purple range are called anthocyanins. These large, complex molecules take a lot of energy to create. Many plants invest in them in springtime to protect young emerging leaves from UV radiation, which can damage newly-minted chlorophyll, especially at low temperatures.

Like medical doctors, botanists sometimes find it hard to make their mouths form the phrase "I don't know." This temporary and selective facial paralysis has afflicted me far too often, and to my shame I've pitched a reasonable but untested reply. Many authorities have said that trees make anthocyanins in the fall to protect leaves from the sun. With practice, some of them have even been able to say it without giggling. This explanation is far too simplistic and riddled with problems.

Renowned as frugal and pragmatic creatures, trees don't spend savings without a dang good reason. It seems far-fetched that trees would use precious energy to protect dying chlorophyll at the same time they're busy making the abscission layers that are killing said chlorophyll. If the "fall suntan lotion" explanation is correct, maples should turn red at roughly the same time, with leaves coloring uniformly through the crown, and in any weather conditions—except freezing, which puts an abrupt end to color change.

If you call me up to inquire why some trees use red and purple in their autumn leaf palette, I'll admit that I don't really—well, actually, it depends on the day. I may just tell you the story about faded laundry on the line.

When Trees Go Over the Hill

Senescence is the decline in vigor that happens to all creatures great and diminutive as they close in on the life expectancy of their species. People my age suddenly find they require glasses to see the phone book. Though I suppose by definition anyone still using a phone book is old enough to need glasses.

The onset of this process varies—you probably know of families whose members retain good health into their 90s, and others where that is not the case. Of course environment is important. Eating and sleeping well, cultivating gratitude, and laughing a lot will help keep us healthier longer. But there comes a point beyond which even the best-preserved specimen can't further delay the end of life.

Trees also go through senescence at different rates. Each species has an approximate lifespan after which no amount of TLC can keep them alive. One of the more popular white-barked birches for landscape planting is the native gray birch. You may love your birch clump, but those trees are old at thirty years, ancient at forty—by the time they double over and kiss the ground in heavy snow or an ice storm, they may be on their way out anyway.

Many of us are aware that poplars as a genus are short-lived. Trembling aspen is usually decrepit at fifty, but its close cousin bigtooth aspen might reach eighty, and eastern cottonwoods, our largest poplar, can live more than a hundred years. Pin cherry declines after twenty to thirty  years, but black cherry lives much longer, often more than a hundred. Paper birch in a good location (i.e., not in a landscape setting) may approach 90.

At the other end of the spectrum are oaks. Bur oak is a massive and picturesque tree which can live eight centuries or more. White oak has similar potential. By comparison, red, pin and black oaks are lightweights, rarely living past four hundred. Beech trees, close relatives of oaks, can also live hundreds of years. Unfortunately, a tiny invasive scale insect coupled with a native fungus are killing beech before they reach mature size. Sugar maples and hickories are other long-lived species.

With a few exceptions, short-lived tree species tend to be shade-intolerant, and are usually pioneer, or early succession, trees. In temperate parts of the world with decent rainfall, just about every piece of open land wants to become a forest.

But woods go through many phases as they move toward a stable system. Succession is the permutation of woodlands as they develop from a beaver meadow or pasture to an endpoint, or climax, community. Once the beavers' pond drains as they move to better feeding grounds, or the farm field is abandoned, a natural order of plant life begins to shape the landscape like a living symphony.

The first trees on the scene are often the fast-growing poplars, whose cottony seeds fly many miles. Birch pips, airy and papery as insect wings, blow in as well. White-footed mice cache pin cherry seeds; deer deposit hawthorn and viburnum in their droppings. As the new canopy matures at seventy feet and blocks out the sky, the forest floor becomes too shady for poplar and cherry seedlings to survive.

Into our intrepid pioneer forest of birch, poplar, cherry and hawthorn fly the helicopter samaras (winged seeds) of sugar, soft, and striped maples. Squirrels cache acorns and conifer seeds. These are long-lived, shade-tolerant species. Seeds germinate, and saplings bide their time in the understory, sometimes for decades, waiting for senescence to play out.

Forty years on, many pioneer trees are in decline, and succumb to insects, stem cankers, root rots, or storm damage. Every time a trembling or bigtooth aspen goes down, a patch of sunlight illuminates the forest floor, allowing a patient, shade-tolerant

66

maple, oak or hemlock to quickly stretch for the sky.

Eventually a stable mix of long-lived, relatively shade-tolerant trees develop, a climax community. The species composition will vary depending on elements such as soil type, slope and climate. Elders will topple every so often, allowing the youngsters a chance at the sun, but the makeup of the forest will remain roughly the same until the next ice age, bulldozer or beaver dam wipes the slate clean.

Neither person nor plant can avoid senescence, which has the same Latin root, *senex*, or old, as senility. In that sense I envy trees. The decline of individual trees is a critical part of the forest life cycle, and they don't have to worry about remembering where they left the car keys, or the car for that matter.

Chapter Three

Wildlife

Just about everyone who saw the Walt Disney classic "Bambi" shed a tear, or at least stifled the urge to lacrimate (that's cry in Scrabble-ese). Even if I had known about the devastating effects deer have on forest regeneration, not to mention crops, landscapes and gardens, it still would have been a trauma for my five-year-old self when Bambi's mother got killed. (Oops—spoiler alert—sorry.) But how might the movie have ended if they had all lived happily ever after?

Deer Grandma and Grandpa

What is life like for those few lucky, possibly smarter, white-tailed deer which manage to avoid cars, coyotes, projectiles and parasites beyond the first few years of existence? Could an aged deer manage to gum your hostas to a nub when its teeth have worn away? I picture a wizened Grand-Buck griping that salt licks were better when he was a fawn, and that yearlings have it easy crossing the road these days now that cars have antilock brakes.

Seriously though, life gets harder in many ways as organisms age. Ask anyone who retired to Florida why they left northern New York and they'll probably tell you winters were enjoyable until arthritis and various other ailments set in. What happens to wild deer as they become senior citizens—do they succumb to age-related health issues like bad joints, decayed teeth, or tumors?

I put the question to retired New York State Department of

Environmental Conservation (NYSDEC) Wildlife Biologist Ken Kogut, who lives outside of Potsdam, NY. He laughed. "To have a deer die of old age in the wild is an oxymoron," he said. Ken went on to explain that in terms of hunting, NYSDEC data show the vast majority of harvested deer are in the 1.5 to 3.5-year-old range—because they are born in May and June, deer are always in a half-year by hunting season. "To see a seven or eight-year-old buck [at a NYSDEC check station] is very, very unusual."

To illustrate this point, consider that the Max Planck Institute for

Demographic Research states the average lifespan of captive white-tails is 16 years, with the confirmed oldest captive deer living to be an ancient 23 years old. Compare that to wild white-tails, which do not have a good track record, so to speak. The average lifespan of a wild deer? According to a University of Michigan report, two years. Yeah. Ten is considered the upper age limit, and a very rare occurrence at that.

Determining the vintage of white-tails is called aging deer, not to be confused with the aging of parents, which is a function of both the number and activity level of their children. How do we find how many birthdays a deer has had? Dentistry.

White-tails have canine teeth, the irony of which, sadly, is lost on them, and incisors on the lower jaw, but none on the upper. In other words they can't snip off a twig the way a rabbit can, but have to tear it away with an upward motion. But they do have upper and lower molars, and the wear on these is used to tell how old a deer is. Or was, as this is generally done post-mortem.

Aging deer started as kind of a home-grown citizen-science project. In years past, keenly observant hunters who could identify an individual deer from yearling stage onward took note of molar wear when it was harvested. Years of correlation of known deer age with measured teeth wear (turns out it's one millimeter per year) made hunters like dairy farmer and NYS Big Buck Club founder Bob Estes of Caledonia, NY, experts in aging white-tails.

Aside from hunting, another thing driving down the average lifespan of wild deer is predation of fawns by coyotes and black bears. Surprisingly, in the Adirondacks, the latter may kill more fawns than coyotes do. Predation is hard to quantify, though, as coyotes and bears eat every last vestige—bone, hair and innards—of any animal they kill or find dead of other causes. Because predators do not feel safe out in the open, they often don't eat carcasses on roadsides, which are left to rot.

Deer-vehicle collisions are another huge factor, with the New York State Department of Transportation reporting an average of 65,000 per year. But starvation during hard winters, says Kogut, is probably the single factor likely to kill older deer. For various reasons including worn molars, they are likely to have less stored body fat going into winter than a younger deer.

With all this carnage, are white-tails disappearing? Hardly. Dr. Peter Smallidge, the State Forester for Cornell Extension, says New York State had an estimated 20,000 deer in the early 1900s, fewer than one deer per two square miles. Today there are a million, over a hundred per square mile in some cases and more than enough to destroy the ability of many forests to regrow.

Lyme disease is also a result of deer overpopulation. Deer do not carry Lyme, but they are very effective incubators of black-legged or deer ticks, which vector the three known species of *Borrelia* spirochete bacteria responsible for Lyme.

Cornell Extension Wildlife Specialist Dr. Paul Curtis believes that if the deer population went down below six per square mile—still higher than the historic density—then deer ticks would become too scarce for Lyme to be a public health threat. What might cause the deer population to decline like that? I don't know, but it certainly won't be old age.

Fall Migrants

It can cruise at an altitude of 29,000 feet, is a beloved icon of the great outdoors, and yet can be the bane of lawn lovers. It's the honking harbinger of advancing autumn and coming cold (and sometimes, of bad alliteration), the Canada goose.

The familiar autumn voices of Canada geese overhead can at once evoke the melancholy of a passing summer and the anticipation of a bracing new season of color and activity. Kids return to school, hunters take to the woods, and farmers work past dusk and into darkness, all to the cacophonous cries and the heartbeat of wings of migrating geese.

Through the end of November and even beyond, waves of airborne athletes—hundreds of thousands in number—will plow their V-shaped squadrons across North Country skies en route from their northern breeding sites to their winter feeding grounds. Canada geese nest in northern Quebec, Ontario,

Labrador and Newfoundland, and winter-over in southern NY State, Pennsylvania and other regions more hospitable than their arctic nests. Depending on how far north they nest, the migrants may cover nearly 1,000 miles each trip.

When stopping for several days to feed at favorable locations along their migration routes, Canada geese will fly low from one feeding ground to the next. They have been documented at nearly 30,000 feet, but during migration they typically fly at about 3,000 feet.

On average, the Canada geese that wing by us twice a year measure between 30-40 inches long with a wingspan of 50-70 inches, and weigh 8.5 pounds. The largest wild Canada goose weighed 24 lbs. and had an 88-inch wingspan, a record among all goose species worldwide. No one claims to fully understand how geese navigate, but being able to sense the Earth's magnetic field seems to be critical. Visual cues, star positioning and even smell may play a role as well.

Among the things that endear Canada geese to us is the fact that they mate for life. From the time they begin breeding at 2 or 3 years old until they succumb to old age 20 or 25 years later, these birds will remain loyal (for the most part) to their mates. Should one member of the pair die, the other usually selects a new partner.

73

According to the Cornell Ornithology Lab, there are eleven subspecies of *Branta canadensis*, the Canada goose, although some authorities only recognize seven. All experts agree, however, that no Canada goose has ever owned a valid Canadian passport even though the species is erroneously called the "Canadian goose" fairly often. The finer points of taxonomic squabbling aside, a more important distinction is the one between migrant and resident geese.

While there's evidence geese no longer fly as far south as they once did due to a changing climate, the journey is still an impressive one. As far as anyone knows, Canada geese have been migrating between their arctic nurseries and temperate wintering grounds for millennia. In contrast, it appears that resident geese are a more recent phenomenon.

A small population of resident Canada geese was documented in New York State in the early 1900s. The New York State Department of Environmental Conservation (NYSDEC) says these were descended from captive birds released downstate by private landowners. As the original population grew and spread, NYSDEC released captive-bred geese in the Albany area in the 1950s and 60s, increasing the resident NYS geese population. NYSDEC reports we now have about 200,000 resident Canada geese in the state.

Unfortunately, geese—especially residents—have become pests in parks, golf courses and home lawns. Being vegetarians, they are happy to take advantage of grass. Their droppings elicit complaints on aesthetic grounds, and because they may be a source of fecal coliform bacteria. And when geese pass overhead, there's a whole new meaning to the phrase "duck, duck—goose."

Also, male geese can sometimes be aggressive as they seek to protect their young. This is especially true during the 4-6 weeks in June and early July when they are unable to fly well because they have molted, and their new feathers are growing in. Balancing the public's love of wildlife with nuisance complaints and potential health risks is a challenge for public officials.

No matter how much of a problem resident waterfowl may become, I will always thrill to the cries of migrating geese in autumn and spring. The poet Mary Oliver sums it up for me in her poem "Wild Geese."

"Whoever you are, no matter how lonely, the world offers itself to your imagination, calls to you like the wild geese, harsh and exciting, over and over announcing your place in the family of things."

Warming Up the Organs to Make Music

Every spring, Mother Nature takes the choir out of the freezer. And sometimes she pops them back in for a while. The choir to which I refer is that all-male horde of early-spring frogs: spring peepers, wood frogs, and chorus frogs. Even while an ice-rind still clings to the pond edges, untold numbers of these guys roust themselves from torpor to sing for female attention.

While in our species it is mostly an inflated ego which causes males to become loud attention-mongers when seeking mates, an inflated vocal sac is what allows male frogs to be so noisy. This air-filled structure balloons out and acts as a resonance chamber to amplify sound. The inflated vocal sac of a peeper is almost as big as the frog itself. This contrasts with the human male, whose ego can sometimes swell to many times his body size.

Spring peepers (*Pseudacris crucifer*) are the most vocal of the trio, and their song is the most widely recognized. I'd describe their call as a sweet, shrill—let's see—peep, shall we say. Singly or in small groups it is melodious, and a large population of them can be deafening, and some people with atypical hearing ranges describe it as painful.

The rough "X" (or cross; hence the species name) on their backs help identify this tan, inch-long amphibian with toe pads similar to those of a tree frog. Peepers can in fact climb trees, but for whatever reason they seldom do. Maybe there is no need to climb because they can

practically fly. Peepers can jump 40 to 50 times their body length.

If it quacks like a duck, it's not always a duck. Wood frogs (*Lithobates sylvaticus*) are plenty vocal, though their calls don't carry as far as other frogs' do. Their call is a short quack, not so much like they are imitating a duck call, but more like they are inspired by it. I have sometimes thought it sounds like barking, but that may be a minority opinion.

As their name indicates, wood frogs spend considerable time in the forest, wintering over in the leaf litter, and breeding in shallow ephemeral pools in the woods. Measuring around 2 ½ inches long, they are brown to copper-colored, with a raccoon-like dark mask across their eyes.

Every time I approach a group of wood frogs in early spring I am tempted to set up a curtain or something so they can have privacy. Let's just say they are rather animated and communal in their business dealings, in addition to being very public. Wood frogs create large collective egg masses, apparently not a common practice in the frog world.

If winter's frost is more than a few inches deep, both spring peepers and wood frogs freeze solid for several months at a time. Obviously they have some kind of super-powers, namely that they pump cellular water outside the cell walls. They also produce antifreeze to help prevent tissue damage at below-freezing temps.

It turns out that among other chemicals, they create ethylene glycol, the same thing you put in your car radiator. If more than a quart of this compound is released into the environment, it's considered a "reportable quantity," and therefore a hazardous spill that must be disclosed to regulators. I don't know how many winterized peepers or wood frogs it would take to constitute a quart of ethylene glycol, but good luck getting them to register with the EPA.

The choir wouldn't be complete without the aptly named chorus frog. Our boreal, or upland, chorus frog (*Pseudacris kalmi*) is one- to 1 ½- inches long, greenish-gray to brown, with three dark stripes down its back. More or less the backup singers for spring peepers, their call is a melodious, trilling "crreeek" that lasts a second or two. Listen for this understated song amidst the nonstop cacophony of peepers.

If you've ever run your fingernail along the teeth of a cheap, hard-plastic comb, you've approximated their call. Go easy on the comb, though, or you may have female chorus frogs following you around.

When dormant animals are roused from torpor several times before spring actually arrives, it is stressful on them. Finding appropriate shelter, in the case of chorus frogs, and preparing to become frog-sicles in the case of peepers and wood frogs, takes energy. Since there is little to eat yet, they are still relying on energy reserves from the previous year. Going back under the spell of the Ice Queen once is probably not an issue, but if it were to happen repeatedly it could cause undue stress.

I Brake for Dinosaurs

Snapping turtles evoke a range of feelings from admiration to fear, but whatever your opinion, you have to respect their

survival skills. Apparently turtles go back some 215 million years, but the snapper we know today has "only" endured for about 40 million years. In a 1993 article in *Smithsonian* magazine, biologist B. Gilbert called them "...creatures who are entitled to regard the brontosaur and mastodon as brief zoological fads."

Physically, snappers haven't changed since prehistoric times, but their world sure has. As far as we can tell from the fossil record, motor vehicles were not a threat back then.

From late May until early July, female snappers are out looking for places to dig a hole in which to deposit their 20-40 leathery

"Ping-Pong ball" eggs, and you may see them busily egg-laying on sandy road shoulders or crossing the pavement. Sadly, many such females, ranging in size from about eight pounds up to thirty or more, are killed by traffic.

Even more tragic is the fact that some motorists intentionally hit snapping turtles, which are unfairly blamed for killing off game fish and young waterfowl. Snapping turtles are omnivores, feeding on everything from aquatic vegetation to crayfish to carrion. During the height of summer the majority of their diet is plant-based.

It's not to say turtles won't eat a bass or gosling, but decades of research from the 1950s to the present day indicate they have no measurable impact on game species. (Private ponds and other non-natural habitats are exceptions and can sometimes require turtle management.) Despite that, they're still seen as a threat to wildlife by a small minority of those who fish and hunt.

A turtle's shell, composed of a carapace (top) and a plastron (bottom) is an extension its vertebrae. As such, it's living bone, though covered in tissue similar in composition to our fingernails. Unfortunately, the shell isn't as strong as it looks, and even if a turtle appears unscathed after being hit by a car, chances are it has numerous broken bones and internal injuries.

You can help a turtle cross the road as long as you follow a few rules. First, be safe. Don't stop if you'll be in danger of getting hit, or of causing a traffic accident. You don't want to get other drivers injured (even if it turns out to be a turtle-hitter). Second, listen to the turtle. If she wants to get across the road, it doesn't matter if you think conditions on the other side don't look conducive to egg-laying. If you turn her back she's just going to cross again.

The safest way to handle a snapping turtle, of course, is to ask someone else to do it. In the water they feel secure, and are generally docile—bites are extremely rare in water. On land, however, it's a different story. Because snappers can't pull themselves inside their shells as completely as other turtles can, they've developed attitude to compensate. Their unusually long necks can reach around nearly to their back legs to snap with their toothless—but sharp—beaks.

Picking up turtles by the tail may seem like a safe method, but this can damage their spines. So put on some heavy leather gloves and grasp the shell on either side about two-thirds of the way back. Careful, though. Remember the part about them reaching back past the middle of their shells to bite? I carry a scoop shovel in the trunk for turtle-herding.

Because road-killed snapping turtles are nearly always fertile females, road mortality is a real threat to their species. Snappers mature by size rather than age, and begin breeding when their shells measure roughly eight inches across. A large female can weigh 25-35 lbs. with a shell of 15"-20" in diameter.

Turtle shells are segmented like a mosaic. Each section, known as a scute, has growth rings that correspond to age, similar to the annual rings of a tree. These rings are how we know snappers in the wild can live at least 70 years, and quite possibly longer, though the average age is closer to thirty.

Slowing down near wetlands during breeding season can help reduce turtle mortality. You're most likely to see snapping turtles during June from dawn to midday, and again in the evening. Also, let's help restore their reputation by spreading the word that they're not a danger to fish and waterfowl. We need to respect our elders, especially those that have been around longer than the dinosaurs.

Porcupines

This fearless animal has an adorable face, plows snow all winter and has a six-million-acre park named after it. One of 29 species worldwide, the North American porcupine (*Erethizon dorsatum*) is the largest New World species, growing to 36 inches long and weighing as much as 35 pounds. That makes it the

second-largest North American rodent behind the beaver, but still puny compared to an African crested porcupine which can exceed 60 pounds. It is also the only cold-hardy porcupine, and one of the few that regularly climb trees.

Its name derives from the Latin for "quill pig," but the Kanien'kehá:ka (Mohawks) call it anêntaks, literally, "bark eater." This is a less-than-endearing term they once applied to the Algonquins living in, well, the Adirondacks. Unlike Mohawks who even back then were expert agronomists with stores of grain and legumes on hand, Algonquins were hunter-gatherers who, by choice or need, would eat the inner bark of pine, maple, elm and other trees. Eventually the Algonquins moved to points north and east, but the place name remained.

Porkies are active all winter, which is a great time to track them.

More or less bullet-shaped, they make effective plows, carving channels through the snow. Since they tend to use the same paths, you can go out after a new snowfall to see which troughs have been cleared in the night. In contrast to most species, our porcupines are not strictly nocturnal, although they do tend to be more active at night.

Porcupine feet are pebbly textured and have no fur, and in deep snow you may also see marks where its tail drags side to side as it waddles. In cases where the claws do not register, its footprint can look (I think) unnervingly like that of a small child. Especially if you're not really awake yet and have stumbled out to the porch for firewood.

Like all porcupines, ours is covered in hair interspersed with up to 30,000 hollow barbed quills. This accounts for their cavalier attitude toward scary stuff like humans, dogs and, unfortunately, cars. Quills are not missiles—they aren't launched at a predator, but they will come off at the drop of a hat, provided you drop it on a porcupine. The barbed ends are amazingly good at sticking to skin and other things. If not removed, quills work their way through flesh, and can be fatal depending on their trajectory.

Quills were and are used the world over by native peoples for embroidering. Usually white at the base and fading to brown and then black at the tips, quills have an innate beauty but are often dyed and worked into leather or textiles. In North America, native peoples reportedly threw a blanket over a porcupine and harvested quills that stuck to it. I have taken quills in a similar way from road-killed porkies with a leather glove.

Most of the time, quills lie flat. When confronted by a predator a porcupine raises them, and keeps its back end to the threat. A porky can lash its eight- to ten-inch-long tail side to side, creating

82

a protective radius around itself. Fishers, fierce predators and one of the largest members of the weasel family, are quick enough to outflank a porcupine and kill it by attacking the quill-free head.

Having a cute face only gets you so far in life, and porcupines are despised by many people because bark-eating damages, or even kills, trees. They are attracted to salt, and will chew on tool handles, canoe paddles or other items handled by people, which doesn't thrill the owners of said objects. One year, a porky found its way under my house and chewed on the sub-floor beneath the kitchen. Who knows, maybe decades ago there was a spill of pickle brine that soaked through.

In addition to eating bark of all kinds, they love herbaceous plants, and are in clover in a field of alfalfa or clover. They have a particular weakness for apples. It is impressive how far out on a branch a porcupine will go to get one, seeming to defy gravity.

Porkies usually den in rock crevices and caves, or sometimes in hollow trees. Breeding is in October and December. In May and June, females may birth up to four young, but generally just one. Not only do they have a low birth rate, it takes more than two years for them to fully mature. In the wild, a porcupine may live 17 or 18 years, with the oldest on record being an ancient 28 years.

A former neighbor of mine, long since passed, had as a young man been given an orphan porcupine. He said it made a great pet, and showed off pictures of a full-size porky in his arms. Kids and adults love to watch porcupines, as they are one of the few wild animals that will stand for such ogling. If there aren't any where you live, maybe you can plan a trip this summer to that northern NY State Park--the "Porcupine" Mountains.

Tench Tensions

You wouldn't think minnows, which seem like benign 1:200 scale models of real fish, would garner complaints. How much trouble can a minnow cause?

Potentially a lot if it's real big and likes to have a crazy-lot of babies. It may be a card-carrying member of the minnow family, but the invasive tench (*Tinca tinca*) can grow to 18 inches long and weigh as much as three pounds. In addition, it has a voracious appetite and will eat literally any organic matter. As for reproduction, experts disagree, but at minimum a female will lay around 200,000 eggs a year, possibly as many as 900,000.

Tench are native to most of Europe, including the British Isles and Nordic countries, and to parts of southwestern Asia as well, but are now present on every continent save Antarctica. Some invasive species need to stow away in pallet wood to get here, but tench were intentionally brought in. As early as 1883, the United States Bureau of Fisheries started shipping them here as a fish farm species.

Experienced anglers will probably find it easier to identify this invader, which can look like a native minnow species when immature. With a deep but thin body, mature tench could be mistaken for a panfish such as rock bass. From above they typically look green, ranging from olive to very dark; this transitions to gold on the sides and belly. They have black fins, rather small red-orange eyes, and tiny scales embedded in an unusually thick film of mucus. For those who don't want to evaluate mucus layers, look for two small barbels ("whiskers"), one on either side of the upper jaw.

They are now established in 38 states, including New York, which has recently identified tench in the Great Chazy River (2008) and Lake Champlain (2002). In Canada they are in British Columbia and also Quebec, where a new hybrid escaped from an unlicensed fish farm into the Richelieu River and eventually the St. Lawrence. To date we know it has reached Montreal, and may have traveled farther. It is the Quebec hybrid strain which currently threatens the Great Lakes and the upstream reaches of the St. Lawrence.

If tench are tasty and we farm-raise them in ponds, what's the problem? One issue is that tench are tolerant to a fault. Except for whitewater conditions and marshes, they're happy whether the waterbody is salt or fresh, flowing or static, clean or polluted, tropical or frigid, oxygenated or anoxic, and—get this—wet or dry (evidently they can survive in mud for several months—exact limit unknown—until a dry spell ends). And although they prefer snails and mollusks, tench will eat whatever, including rotting vegetation. They make carp and suckers look persnickety.

Being laid-back about what you eat and where you sleep is not necessarily a problem, as many college students will attest to. Bad habits are another matter. Fact: poor table manners may lead to reduced water quality.

Gregarious, boisterous diners, tench churn up bottom sediments, which increases turbidity and releases nutrients from the mud.

Tench also harbor parasites that can be transferred to native fish and mollusks. The copper redhorse (*Moxostoma hubbsi*) is said to be particularly vulnerable. Tench compete with indigenous fish such as perch, and have been associated with a decline of that species following their invasion of a waterbody. Mollusks and crustaceans, organisms which consume algae, are preferentially grazed by tench to the point that algae blooms may occur more frequently post-infestation.

Not all invasive species are created equal. The Asian longhorn beetle (ALB) seems like the project of an evil overlord. If ALB has one redeeming quality, no one has yet identified it. Tench, on the other hand, have some supporters. Easily raised under all kinds of conditions, they are an important food source, and are still cultivated around the world (including in one US state). They are considered a decent sport fish in some locales, and are fodder for many native fish.

Perhaps because of its equivocal character, widespread distribution and long history of domestication, tench has not been studied as much as other aquatic invasives have. Tench may not be as destructive as some invaders, but we know it will cause some degree of harm to the Great Lakes ecosystem, and we need to do all we can to exclude it for as long as possible.

White-Nose Syndrome

Context is critical. Years ago I took a second job loading trucks at night, and a few guys on the dock had what you might call "white-nose syndrome." All I had was coffee to keep awake, so they worked faster than I, though they spent a lot more time in the rest room. I hope they eventually recovered.

Addiction is a serious and potentially life-threatening matter, but from a bat's perspective, white-nose syndrome (WNS) is something even more devastating. This disease, which is nearly always fatal, has killed 80% of the bats in the Northeastern U.S. in less than a decade. Initially found in central New York in 2007, white-nose syndrome now affects bats in 28 states and 6 Canadian provinces. Since it was first identified, it has felled more than 7 million bats, leaving once-packed hibernation sites, or hibernacula, empty, and pushing some species to the edge of extinction.

The disease is caused by a cold-loving fungus, *Pseudogymnoascus destructans*, which attacks hibernating bats. Its common name comes from the fuzzy white fungal growth that develops on the muzzle and wings of infected bats. Because *Pseudogymnoascus* is only active between 40 and 60 degrees F, and prefers very high humidity, it does not affect bats in their summer roosts.

The fungus is not native to North America, and researchers believe it was introduced by caving enthusiasts from abroad on their clothing or gear, likely several years before its discovery. Research has shown that the fungus remains viable on clothing for long periods of time. It was initially thought the pathogen originated in Europe, but scientists now say it's unclear whether it came from Asia or Europe.

After its introduction in a high-traffic commercial cave in Schoharie County, NY, white-nose syndrome quickly spread via bat-to-bat contact, and by contact with spores on contaminated surfaces in hibernacula. Fortunately, it does not appear to spread through the air.

According to Benjamin Tabor of New York State Department of Environmental Conservation's Bureau of Wildlife, it is not the disease itself that kills bats, but rather the changes in behavior it induces. Tabor explains that the white-nose pathogen irritates the skin of infected bats. They wake from torpor to scratch their muzzles, and then often fly about in confusion before returning to "power-saver mode." Hibernating bats pack a modest winter picnic in the form of fat reserves to sustain them until spring. Rousing a half-dozen times during winter to scratch their faces and fly around burns off bats' energy reserves too soon, and they starve to death.

New York, possibly the state hardest hit by WNS, is home to six kinds of cave bats: the little brown, big brown, northern, tricolor, Indiana and long-eared. Cave bats are most at risk because they hibernate in dense clusters in caves or mines that are contaminated with WNS spores. New York also has three types of tree bats, but these are less susceptible to white-nose syndrome. The more solitary behavior of tree bats, as well as the fact their hibernation sites are much drier than those of cave bats, protect them from the disease.

Body size seems related to mortality, with smaller species dying off in greatest numbers. Once the most numerous species in NY State, the little brown bat population has declined by over 90% since 2008. Populations of northern bats and tricolor bats have also plummeted, down 98% in both species. The big brown bat, the largest NYS species, has fared somewhat better, with a decline of around 50 percent.

Along with spiders and snakes, bats are one of God's creatures which seem to trigger an innate fear response in many people. Stories about vampires in folklore and popular culture don't exactly help endear bats to us, either. But if you dislike mosquitoes, especially given what we know about the Zika and West Nile viruses, you might learn to appreciate bats a little more.

Fortunately, all bats in our region eat flying insects exclusively. In fact they consume up to 50% of their body weight each day in critters that may have a taste for human blood. Reportedly, each little brown bat eats more than 1,000 insects per hour at night.

And they take a serious bite out of the agricultural pest population. According to the United States Geological Survey National Wildlife Health Center, insect suppression by bats saves the US agriculture industry (including forestry) a minimum of $4 billion, and possibly as much as $50 billion, annually.

For more information about WNS, contact your local New York State Department of Environmental Conservation office. Also, stay out of caves where bats are hibernating, and keep your nose clean.

Beavers

Among the myriad
blessings in my life are
good neighbors. Over the
years they have come
through with everything
from a jump-start on a
cold morning to a cup of
sugar in the midst of pie-
making. They've even
delivered and stacked
firewood when I was ill for
an extended time.

Some years ago I was concerned when a new family built a house
right next door, almost overnight, without warning or even a
building permit. They were hard workers, to be sure, and could
fell timber like there was no tomorrow, but were very stand-
offish, and I began to eye them with suspicion. Once it was
brought to my attention they were beavers, we got along much
better.

The North American beaver (*Castor canadensis*) has superior fur
than does the species (*Castor fiber*) found in Europe and Asia.
But it doesn't always pay to be the best. Once nearly extirpated
from this continent to satisfy demand for its castor—oily goo
from its anal glands prized for use in perfume and medicine—and
its lustrous fur, our native beaver has made a remarkable
comeback in the past 50 years.

This population rebound is great for improved water quality and
groundwater storage, healthier fisheries, habitat diversification,

and more migratory waterfowl. It is not such good news when beaver and human engineering clashes, as happened one morning when I found that a stream, usually directed under my dirt road, was suddenly flowing over it and washing away the roadbed at quite a clip.

Humans and beavers alter their environment more drastically and much faster than other animals are able to do. The difference is that beavers are not generally subject to building codes or property taxes for their lodges, or required to file environmental impact statements for dams. While many of our dams are for hydro power, some are for safety—downstream flood control. Beavers also construct dams for safety, but in a different sense.

At home in the water but awkward on land, they are more vulnerable to predation by coyotes, fishers and wolves up in "dry dock." Basically they landscape with water, a kind of beaver *feng shui*. In addition to building dams to create ponds, they dig canals to extend their reach beyond the shoreline.

Beavers are sort of like ducks in the back, but raccoons up front. They have webbed hind feet for swimming, but agile forepaws for making mud pies (they do not really move mud with their tails). Other aquatic adaptations include a 15-minute dive time, and having a second pair of lips behind their teeth for chewing underwater. They also have a set of transparent inner eyelids which act like goggles, suggesting that prehistoric water may have been chlorinated on a regular basis.

On average, beavers measure about 3.5 feet in length, including an 8 to 12-inch tail, and weigh roughly 45 pounds, though they have been known to exceed 100 pounds. This makes them the biggest rodent in North America. If animals this size can build dams that range from a few yards to more than 2,700 feet long, imagine what it was like in the Pleistocene with *Castoroides*, giant six-foot-long beavers that weighed 200 pounds or more. It must have been tough to be a nuisance-wildlife control officer back then.

Given the way beavers can knock down a 12" hardwood tree overnight, it is not surprising they have carbide-tipped teeth. Well almost—the enamel in the front of their incisors is reinforced with high concentrations of iron. This means the back always wears more, giving the tooth a perfect chisel shape. They gnaw wood to fell trees and to get building material, but bark is their main food.

Besides bark, beavers munch on twigs, buds and leaves of various trees; favorites are birch, aspen, willow, and maple. Because they do not hibernate, they store loads of tasty tree parts underwater in the bottom sediments. Pond-lily tubers are relished, though I don't know where they get the relish. Also, they have been seen rolling up lily pads like cigars and eating them, presumably because they find the green cheroots difficult to light.

Exemplars of family values, beavers are monogamous for life, which translates to maybe a 10-year marriage between first mating at 2 or 3 years and death at the ripe age of 12 or 13, besting the 8.2-year average length of marriage in the U.S. And they have a modicum of gender equality—both male and female beavers help raise their offspring. Social bonds are strong, with up to three generations living together. Older siblings frequently pitch in to groom or babysit the young kits. Beavers of all ages, especially yearlings and kits, engage in play. This is one of the reasons many Native American peoples refer to beavers as "Little

People," and hold them in high esteem.

Apparently the sound of running water is their cue to check for breaches in dams. Researchers played a recording of a babbling brook next to a beaver lodge, and most of the inhabitants went right out to check the dam. (I imagine the rest of them had to excuse themselves to go empty their bladders.)

Even though they may have the moral high ground when it comes to social issues, beavers can be annoying neighbors. I had to fence off young fruit trees from beaver damage, and modify their dam so the yard did not flood. Solutions can be simple, like an "over-under" pipe that lets them build the dam as tall as they want while leaving the water level where you want it. Beavers are not aggressive, though an adult can hold its own against a dog when cornered.

For help resolving conflicts with local beavers, call your local NYS Department of Environmental Conservation or USDA Soil and Water Conservation District office. For issues with human neighbors, sorry; you're on your own.

Long Time, No Sea

I'm all for gender integration and parity, but quite often, gulls and buoys just don't go together. While it's true most gulls spend much or all of their lives near salt water, some, notably the

ring-billed gull, live hundreds if not thousands of miles inland and may never see the sea.

Worldwide there are about fifty species of gulls, often called seagulls. They range in size from the little gull (kudos there for description, if not creativity), weighing about four ounces, to the great black-backed gull which tips the scale at four pounds. They can be found the world over from the high arctic to Antarctica, although they are less numerous in tropical areas.

Gulls are monogamous, having a single mate for life except for rare "divorces" (for which they pay a social price). Colonial breeders, they return to the same site year after year. In a twist of gender roles, a few males will provide daycare for a colony's developing chicks while other adults are out getting food. Males also take turns with females to incubate eggs.

While gulls may have a tiny noggin, they are by no means bird-brained. Fast learners, they adapt to all sorts of new environments and are quick to exploit novel food sources. Technically speaking, gulls are opportunistic omnivores. This means they're on a "see-food" diet—if they see food, they eat it.

If necessary they'll catch and eat everything from fish and mollusks to rodents and earthworms, but they would prefer a handout. If begging doesn't work, they scavenge and steal like the pros they are. You can find them in fields following behind a plow or manure spreader to see what tasty morsels turn up. Beaches, parking lots and dumpsters all have riches to offer a sharp-eyed gull.

Unfortunately, the only time a lot of us take notice of gulls is when they are being a nuisance. Besides stealing French fries, they carry garbage from landfills to nearby properties, and damage buildings when they site large nesting colonies atop roofs. By and large, though, gulls serve an important role cleaning up messes, natural and human-made, with a little hunting and fishing in their spare time.

Gulls seem plentiful, but may be under threat if a recent trend continues. Since 1963 when Type E botulism was first identified in the Great Lakes, sporadic incidents have resulted in fish and bird kills. However, beginning in 2006, frequent and widespread botulism outbreaks have caused unprecedented die-offs, killing tens of thousands of gulls, loons, herons, cormorants, mergansers and other species.

The fall of 2014 was especially bad, with hundreds of waterfowl washing ashore at a time on the lower great Lakes, including Lake Ontario. Apparently, several invasive aquatic species, the round goby in particular, are to blame for this escalation.

New York State is home to four breeding gull species: the great black-backed, herring, ring-billed, and laughing gulls. Quite a few additional species pass through the State during migrations, especially on Lake Champlain, the St. Lawrence River and the mid- to lower Hudson River. Less-common species such as Franklin's gull or the visually striking ivory gull may mix in with resident species.

The two gulls you're most likely to encounter are the herring and ring-billed. The most common gull on the Atlantic coast, herring gulls are stout gray-and-white birds with pink legs, generally seen squabbling over picnic remains or whatever the tide brought in. For some reason, herring gulls in the UK have gotten especially cranky, and in the summer of 2015 were reported to have injured people and pets, killing a tortoise and two small dogs. (Eat your heart out, Alfred Hitchcock.)

Ring-billed gulls are smaller than herring gulls, with thinner bills having—no surprise—a dark band encircling them. These medium-size gulls are ubiquitous throughout the Great Lakes region as well as in the Midwest. Like most gulls, they migrate in winter, but often to the mid-Hudson or other open fresh water, not the ocean. Even having a life far removed from the sea, the ring-billed gull seems nonetheless happy as a clam.

Hibernation

The deadly sin of one individual may be the life-saving virtue of another. I'm not a big proponent of envy, anger, and gluttony, but sloth is different. The lives of some organisms depend on being able to sleep for half the year, a fact which I tried,  unsuccessfully, to conceal from my kids. Woodchucks, bats, ground squirrels and many other animals have survival strategies which include long bouts of sloth. Ironically, actual sloths do not hibernate.

In general terms, hibernation is a state of inactivity and lowered metabolism among warm-blooded animals (endotherms) during winter. This of course describes the condition of many of us from early January through March, so there's a bit more to it than that. Exactly what, however, is up for debate, as biologists have long argued what counts as hibernation.

It used to be applied only to species which entered profound dormancy, for example certain Arctic rodents whose heart rates drop to a tiny fraction of their summer values, and whose internal temperatures fall below freezing in their winter dens. But that club was thought too exclusive, and these days the term is applied to any animal having the means to actively lower their metabolism and body temperature. I'd say actively lowering one's metabolism sounds like an oxymoron, but I'll refrain from name-calling.

Cold-blooded animals (ectotherms) like frogs and snakes also become dormant in winter. It's basically the same as hibernation but biologists call it brumation. With ectotherms, you might say hibernation just happens; it's not something that they "do." Even though they don't have to work hard at sleeping the way mammals do, their torpor is impressive in its own way. Some frogs, turtles and fish can overwinter in mud that is essentially devoid of oxygen, and as far as we know they're no worse for the wear, come spring.

Most hibernators tailor their schedules based on the weather—if it stays mild into late fall, black bears and chipmunks will den up later than usual. But some critters, known as obligate hibernators, doze off according to the calendar. Even if you sent a European hedgehog to Aruba for a winter vacation, it would go narcoleptic at the same time as its mates back in the Scottish Highlands fell asleep.

Bears are one of those creatures which didn't make the hibernator list in the old days, but which are now lumped in with Arctic popsi-squirrels and other high-latitude rodents in the frozen-mammals section. Bears in the far north may not freeze, but they do not eat or drink for up to eight months, using stored fat for hydration and energy. If we were inert for that long our muscles would waste away, but bears have processes to manage proteins such that their muscles don't atrophy.

As long as temperatures don't fall sharply, many insects survive winter by making antifreeze, various glycols which keep ice from forming inside their cells. Unlike honeybees, all members of wild bee and wasp colonies die in autumn except a few mated queens. Some of these overwinter alone, but others gather in large numbers in sheltered hibernacula. One fall I had to tear down an exterior brick chimney, and more than a hundred frozen paper-wasp queens poured out from a pocket behind it. (I bedded them in straw, and they all woke up in April.)

In hot climates, summer is the unbearable season, and some animals sit it out by hibernating, except that's not what it's called. Estivation is the proper term for hot-weather snoozing. Some desert-dwelling frogs surround themselves with a mucus "water balloon" to wait out dry spells. African lungfish have a similar trick for when their ponds temporarily dry up. More surprising is that at least one estivator is a primate—the fat-tailed Madagascar dwarf lemur sleeps in a hollow tree for half the year until the heat's off.

If a close relative of ours can go dormant, then what about us? In some sci-fi movies, astronauts wake after years of travel, which may be another case of what was once imagined becomes real. In 2014, NASA announced that they're looking for a means to place the crews of multi-year space missions into suspended animation for three to six months at a time. Presumably this is so Mission Control won't have to listen to incessant "Are we there yet?" whining from the back of the spaceship.

Though stories of human hibernation abound, documented cases are rare. Occasionally someone falls through ice and is revived hours later with no evident brain damage or other long-term effects. This can occur when body temperature drops very fast, as it would if submerged in ice water, or buried in a snowbank as happened in 2001 to a Canadian toddler who recovered from a near-freezing body temperature with no apparent ill effects.

If the body cools slowly, hypothermia usually results, ending in death if continued. Apparently, there are exceptions. One instance happened in 2006 when an injured hiker spent three frigid weeks on Mount Rokko in western Japan with no food or water. His temperature had fallen to about 24C. He also made a full recovery.

Scientists will continue to study hibernation for its medical applications. But if you're not a fan of winter, don't pretend to hibernate by being slothful, just grin and, you know, bear it.

Magnificent Migrants

With all due respect to synchronized swimmers, a flock of up to a million blackbirds turning and wheeling in unison is even more impressive. Although grackles, cowbirds and the invasive starlings are lumped into the category of blackbird, it's our native red-winged blackbird that I more often see.

Considering that red-wing blackbirds are the most numerous bird species in North America, how come their migration often escapes our notice? After all, their flocks are much larger, in terms of numbers, than those of geese. In fact, Richard A. Dolbeer of the USDA-APHIS Wildlife Services in Denver says that a single flock may contain over a million birds.

Canada geese migration is hard to miss. Even if their V-shaped flocks don't catch your eye, their loud honking will let you know what's up, so to speak. But blackbirds are smaller and migrate primarily at night, plus they don't have the pipes that geese have, and their voices don't carry as far. And admittedly they aren't as numerous in northern NY as they are in the upper Midwest.

All blackbirds, red-wings included, are omnivores. They feed on insect pests such as corn earworms, as well as on weed seeds, facts which should endear them to us. Unfortunately, they sometimes eat grain, which has the opposite effect. Studies indicate they seldom cause significant damage to crops.

Along with robins, they're one of the first signs of spring. Usually I hear them before I see them; the males' "oak-a-chee" call is music to my ears in more ways than one. And the red and yellow wing patches, or epaulets, of the males are a welcome splash of color in the sepia-and-snow tones that characterize mid-March.

Red-wings often nest in loose colonies in marshes. I recall canoeing with my young daughter through cattails, peering into red-wing blackbird nests while adults hovered overhead, objecting loudly and sometimes diving a bit too close to our heads. Marshes afford red-wings some protection from predators like foxes and raccoons, and the females, which are a mottled brown, blend in well. Hawks, and owls to a lesser extent, take a toll on blackbirds regardless of where they nest, though.

In the fall, blackbirds flock together before migrating to locations in the southern US. This is when they display their avian acrobatics. Perhaps you've driven along great undulating flocks of blackbirds and marveled at the way they're able to all change course instantly.

One time, a plethora of red-wings descended on a big sugar maple in the yard. I watched in awe as they streamed up out of that maple and poured themselves back down into another one nearby. They repeated this "avian hourglass" performance several times.

Researchers have long puzzled over synchronized flock movement. In recent years they've made some progress thanks to high-speed imaging, algorithms and computer modeling. Movie animators have used these algorithms to depict movements of fish and herd animals.

Apparently, each bird keeps track of its six—no more, no fewer—closest neighbors, and coordinates its movements with them. No matter how many times they turn or dive, they maintain about the same distance between themselves and the six closest birds.

But precisely how do birds maintain distances within a flock, or know when to change course? In the words of Claudio Carere, an Italian ornithologist deeply involved in studying starling flock behavior in Rome, "The exact way it works no one knows." I like an honest researcher.

Winter Survival Tips: Bird-Brained Ideas

During prolonged winter deep-freeze periods, it's hard to believe vacationers flock to northern NY State for its warmth. When the mercury (or whatever that red stuff is in today's thermometers) drops down and stays there a while, several arctic and sub-arctic bird species shift southward to "tropical" climes such as ours.

The first time I saw a gray jay, I thought a blue jay must have gone through the wash with a little bleach. Dark gray above with a lighter belly, the bird also known as the camp-robber, Canada jay or whiskey-jack is about the size of a blue jay, but a little more puffy-looking and lacking a head crest. They're cute as a button, and will eat from your hand if you let them.

Be careful; gray jays are in the crow family, a clever and highly curious clan. They'll graduate from eating crumbs out of hand to nicking your sandwich or even flying into the kitchen if the door's open a bit too long (happened to me). Still, they're adorable, and I love seeing them.

Red crossbills aren't as bold, and since you won't find them hanging around your compost pile or kitchen door, you're less likely to encounter them. Native to boreal spruce-fir forests, they specialize in extracting seeds from cones. I've seen them on Adirondack roadsides, presumably picking up grit, and once stopped to examine a road-killed specimen.

If you're fortunate enough to spot a crossbill, you might think it's in need of an orthodontist. As their name implies, crossbills have a lower beak, or mandible, that crosses to either the right or left (in equal numbers, I'm told) of the upper one. This helps them pry apart the scales of cones to winkle out the seeds that lie between scales.

In sub-zero conditions it seems nothing's more uncomfortable than cold feet. Two birds of prey that visit us in winter, the snowy owl and the rough-legged hawk, have found a solution. In addition to vacationing here in the "warm" south, their other secret to surviving winter is to sprout feathers on their toes.

As you drive along northern roads this winter you may notice (in between whiteouts) hawks perched on utility poles and in trees, hunting rodents and rabbits. If you're lucky you may see one hover or even swoop down on prey. A fair percentage of these are rough-legged hawks. A lot of red-tail hawks, our most abundant hawk species, go farther south during winter.

One of the largest hawks, rough-leggeds have wingspans of 50 to 60 inches, and are one of only two hawk species to have home-grown down boots. Their plumage pattern varies a lot, but generally their wings are white underneath with some dark areas close to the body and possibly dark wingtips. They have one or two dark bands near the tip of an otherwise white tail.

One of the most picturesque and recognizable winter visitors is the snowy owl. The male is nearly pure white, while the larger female has brown scalloping on her chest. Juveniles have dark brown barring. Like most owls, snowies have feathers right to the ends of their toes.

On their native arctic tundra, snowy owls feed mostly on small rodents. But because they're the heaviest owl species, they can take down good-size prey, including ducks, geese, muskrats and raccoons.

Maybe we could learn some tricks from these hardy vacationers. Wear down-filled clothing, including boots. Definitely go south for the winter. Mooching food from neighbors is optional.

Groundhogs

Researchers are still puzzling over the age-old question, "How much wood could a woodchuck chuck if a woodchuck could chuck wood," but I may have an answer. Re-brand the woodchuck.

Like the words skunk and moose, woodchuck (wojak) is a Native American term, Algonquin in this case. I don't know its literal translation, but I suspect it means "fat fur-ball that can inhale your garden faster than you can say Punxsutawney Phil." Or something pretty close to that.

Too bad that to English speakers, the name woodchuck implies the critters are employed in the forest-products industry. They haven't the teeth for chewing wood, nor do they have any use for wood in their burrows. (Exhaustive studies have concluded woodchuck dens aren't paneled.)

Much as I respect the origin of "woodchuck," I'm in favor of sticking to one of its other names, groundhog, which is more descriptive. Not only do these rotund herbivores reside underground, they're such gluttons that I'm pretty sure even swine call them hogs. Tellingly, another moniker is "whistle-pig," referring both to groundhogs' warning call and their voracious appetites.

Native to most of North America from southern Alaska to Georgia, groundhogs are a type of rodent called a marmot. They're related to other marmots and to ground squirrels out west, but in the northeast they have no close kin. Given what a marmot can eat, that's a mercy.

They may be gluttons, but they're not lazy. Groundhogs dig extensive burrows up to 5' deep and 40' long, each having two to five entrances. Supposedly, the average groundhog moves 35 cubic feet of soil excavating its burrow. (I'd like to know who gets the groundhogs to fill up those measuring cups.)

Mature groundhogs in wilderness areas typically measure 15-25" long and weigh 5-9 lbs. Given access to lush gardens or tasty alfalfa, though, they can reach 30" long and weigh as much as 30 lbs. Now that's a ground *hog*. Needless to say, their habit of vacuuming up fields and gardens has given them a bad name in some circles.

Leaf rustling is bad enough, but this hole-digging hobby really riles farmers. Groundhog holes and soil piles can injure livestock, weaken foundations and damage equipment. Many a farmer trying to mow hay has cursed the groundhog when the haybine "finds" a soil pile. Hard to appreciate their cuteness while you replace cutterbar knives for the third time in a day.

True hibernators, groundhogs usually den up in October, their winter body temperature dropping to 50F and their heart slowing to a few beats per minute. Groundhogs might emerge in February in Pennsylvania, but up north you won't find one blearily sniffing around for a mate that early. In the southern Adirondacks in late March I once saw a burrow entrance with a halo of dirt scattered on the snow from where the critter had recently burst out, a squint-eyed dust mop looking for love. Who knows if it went back in for a nap after seeing winter had not yet departed.

The notion that sun on February 2 means a late spring began in ancient Europe. That date marks the pagan festival of Imbolc, halfway between winter solstice and spring equinox. Imbolc was supplanted by Candlemas as Christianity spread, but both traditions reference the "sunny equals more winter, and cloudy means spring" idea.

Mostly because Europe lacked groundhogs, Groundhog Day was invented in the New World, first popping up among Pennsylvania Germans in the mid-1800s. Though Punxsutawney Phil was the original prognosticating marmot, others like Wiarton Willie in Wiarton, Ontario, Jimmy the Groundhog in Sun Prairie, Wisconsin, and General Beauregard Lee of Lilburn, Georgia followed.

We know how much ground a groundhog can hog: a lot, especially if beans and peas are growing on said ground. I say we pull those researchers off the perennial Woodchuck-Chucking Quantification Project and have them find a way to ensure that Groundhog Day is overcast so we can get an early dismissal from winter.

Birds and Bees 2.0

I once heard a quote to the effect that our children help us finish growing up. I do feel I've learned more from my kids than they likely have from me. Patience, acceptance, a shift of perspective as to what is important in life—those are but a few of the lessons my children instilled in me. But it was a real surprise that my son taught me a thing or two on the birds and bees.

A number of times he brought college friends home to visit, including one who did not identify as any gender. I was asked to use the pronouns *they, their,* and *them* when referring to them. This was new, and confusing: if my son spoke of bringing home company, I wasn't sure if "they" meant a crowd, or his non-binary friend.

Lesson two nearly got me killed on my son's campus. As a favor, I diagnosed his roommate's car, pointing out that a leaky return line was the source of his tranny problems. A passer-by overheard this and confronted me, enraged. Luckily she accepted my Old Guy defense; that I had no clue "tranny," which meant transmission when I was a kid, was an offensive term for transgendered people. (Afterwards, my son explained transgender...)

While having no fixed gender or switching later in life is not very common among humans, it is the norm in large swaths of the natural world.

Recently I taught a botany class, and mentioned that ash trees are usually either pollen-bearing male trees or flower-bearing females. But if gender ratios in a certain locale are skewed—for example if female trees are relatively scarce—some of the male trees become females, permanently. This is because ash trees are polygamo-dioecious. A few of the students thought polygamo-dioecious sounded sketchy, but I assured them it is legal in all 50 states.

This got me thinking about other creatures which start out as one sex, but later switch to another. Turns out this is a popular pastime in the marine world. Clownfish are a great example, with the males very often becoming females when they get older. (I assume this is why *Finding Dory* came after *Finding Nemo*.) They don't just take on the behavior of females, they actually develop ovaries and reproduce as females.

It can go the other way, too. Wrasse are fish which stake out coral reefs, trying to find Nemo, Dory, or any other clownfish to eat. Female wrasse often change into males, but unlike with clownfish, they can change back. It is an example of protogynous hermaphroditism. And also of females changing their mind a lot. I won't even start on which kinds of animals routinely adopt the behavior of the opposite sex, because the list includes nearly all species, including primates.

Invertebrates such as worms, slugs, and snails are typically hermaphrodites, with each individual having both male and female characteristics. There is a species of mollusk called *Crepidula fornicata*, or common slipper shell, which pile on top of one another in a precarious tower to, you know—visit with their upstairs and downstairs neighbors. At the same time.

A few earthworms, and many insects, are parthenogenic, which has nothing to do with worshiping at the Temple of Athena. It means they are females who have figured out how to make babies without the fuss and muss of having to deal with guys. In parthenogenesis, females give birth only to other females, and so on down the line. If you've ever had scale insects on a houseplant, chances are they were all female. Makes it easy for one to go off and found a whole new empire single-handedly. A figurative hand, of course. Snakes, salamanders, sharks, and a few other vertebrate species do this, too, although it seems to be a temporary thing with many of them.

In an ironic twist to the clichéd (and horribly flawed) "birds and bees" metaphor for explaining sexuality, researchers have found that birds as well as bees can be parthenogenic and hermaphroditic. To my knowledge, though, not both at the same time.

The more we learn about the natural world, the more we find that things we had assumed were rare or aberrant are in fact remarkably common. And that clearly they are created in such fashion—clownfish do not choose a lifestyle or decide to switch preferences. And as my kid once pointed out to me, primates like humans can be a bit complex too.

If you have children, hopefully you'll be lucky enough to get a "Birds and Bees" talk from one of them someday when they grow up. You can really learn a lot.

Forget About Reforestation

"Squirrels have been criticized for hiding nuts in various places for future use and then forgetting the places. Well, squirrels do not bother with minor details like that. They have other things on their mind, such as hiding more nuts where they can't find them." Unfortunately, that was penned in 1949 by Will Cuppy in his book *How to Attract the Wombat*. I say unfortunately because I wanted to write it first, but was unable to get born in time.

Before learning stuff like "facts" about squirrels, it made me feel smug to think that their attention span was even worse than mine. Popular wisdom used to hold that the fluffy-tailed rodents spent half their lives burying nuts, only to forget about most of them a few minutes later. I figured that was why they generally seemed frantic, always thinking they hadn't stored any food yet.

The great thing about the whole affair is that tons of butternuts, oaks, hickories and walnuts get planted each fall, mostly in flower boxes it seems, but some in actual forests. As a kid I would see hordes of squirrels in parks, on college campuses and around dumpsters, but few in the woods. The latter, I had assumed, were lost.

So it came as a surprise to learn gray squirrels are native to temperate hardwood forests, at home in large unbroken tracts of woods. In fact, squirrels are critical to the survival of many nut-bearing trees. Walnuts, acorns and hickory nuts, which do not tend to waft on the breeze all that well, and which soon dry out and degrade on the ground, need someone to cart them off and plant them in the soil.

Biologists consider black squirrels a "melanistic subgroup" of the eastern gray squirrel; same species, different shade of gray. (Probably the fifty-first.) Reportedly, black squirrels are far more cold-hardy than their lighter cousins, and their color gives them

110

an advantage in mature forests.

The irony is that while gray squirrels can be so numerous in the human domain that they become pests, they are disappearing from the forests that depend on them for regeneration. The reason is that most woodlands today are patchwork. In a shocking failure of the free market, it seems no one is making large contiguous tracts of hardwood forest any more, even though they're increasingly rare.

It's hard to criticize agriculture, especially if you eat on a regular basis, but clearing land to grow food has fragmented our woods. One problem with breaking up forest land is that animals may need more than just a piece of it at a time.

Gray squirrels have large, shared territories with no real borders. Although they are great at things like planting trees and eating the faces off Halloween pumpkins, they're not so good at running across fields to the next patch of trees. Well the running works OK, but not the looking out for predators. Gray squirrels evolved in a world where hiding places grew on trees. As a result, predation was low. But since the time they have been forced to hike out in the open, hawks, coyotes and foxes have taken a bite out of wild squirrel populations.

Red squirrels, however, are moving into habitats once occupied by gray squirrels. It seems logical to think that an army of red, fluffy nut-planters would be just as good at propagating an oak-hickory forest as the gray, fluffy sort were. Not so. The reds, which evolved among conifers, are accustomed to stashing pine, spruce and fir cones in tree cavities or right out in the open. When they encountered acorns and nuts, they carried on with this tradition. In the open-air caches of red squirrels, tree nuts desiccate and become non-viable. Nothing gets planted. Also, red

111

squirrels have smaller, discrete territories they do not share, so they're not as apt as the grays to gallivant over to a nearby block of woods, and thus they avoid pesky carnivores. In this way they're better adapted to a fragmented forest than the grays are.

Getting back to forgetfulness, science has polished up the reputation of gray squirrels by observing them. Evidently no one thought of doing this novel procedure until 1990. That's when Lucia F. Jacobs and Emily R. Lyman of Princeton University's Biology department set up a series of nut-caching experiments with gray squirrels. And hopefully a few interns as well. Their impressive article was published in the *Journal of Animal Behavior* in 1991, and is readily available online in case anyone has an attention span longer than.

I should mention that gray squirrels are considered "scatter hoarders," stashing nuts and acorns all over the place. They tend to dig them up and rebury them as many as five times prior to winter, possibly to confound greedy neighbors or pilfering jays, or because of anxiety. Each successive re-cache takes them farther and farther from the parent tree, which is good in terms of forest ecology.

Jacob and Lyons concluded that even after waiting 12 days, gray squirrels quickly located about 2/3 of the nuts they buried, but that they also exhumed a few that weren't theirs. However, each squirrel managed to end with at least 90% of the original number provided by researchers. This shows that memory is the primary means of locating cached tree nuts. And that while they don't plant as many trees as we once thought, they make up for it by planting each one many times.

Chapter Four

Plant Life

Everything is edible once. It's good to know which wild plants and fungi you can eat and live to tell about it, which are good medicine, and which ones to avoid.

Call the Dogs off the Lions

Spring showers bring May flowers, but not all posies are a welcome sight. Although it is quite possible they arrived on the Mayflower, dandelions do not get the esteem they deserve as plucky immigrants that put down firm roots in a new land, or as a vitamin-packed culinary delight, or as a multipurpose herbal remedy.

On this latter point, dandelion is so well-respected that it garnered the Latin name *Taraxicum officinale*, which roughly means "the official remedy for disorders." There are many reported health benefits of dandelion, including as a liver support and for alleviating kidney and bladder stones, as well as externally as a poultice for skin boils. I don't pretend to know

113

every past and present medicinal use of the plant, and I strongly recommend consulting a respected herbalist, as well as your health care provider, before trying to treat yourself.

That said, the University of Maryland Medical Center has devoted an entire web page to dandelion, and it cites some peer-reviewed studies. I had previously heard that dandelion was used as an adjunct diabetes treatment, but had not found any references. However, the U of M Medical Center states that

> "Preliminary animal studies suggest that dandelion may help normalize blood sugar levels and lower total cholesterol and triglycerides while raising HDL (good) cholesterol in diabetic mice. Researchers need to see if dandelion will work in people. A few animal studies also suggest that dandelion might help fight inflammation."

I'd say that's not bad for a weed. You can buy dried and chopped dandelion root in bulk or in capsule form at most health-food stores, or you can get it for free in your back yard, providing you don't use lawn chemicals.

Dandelion's common name comes from the French "dent de lion," or lion's tooth, referring to the robust serrations along their leaves. Leaves vary widely in appearance, though, and aside from their yellow mane, not every dandelion is as leonid as the next. Apparently, the French have a corner on the common-name market, because the other dandelion moniker is "pis en lit," or "wet the bed," as the dried root is strongly diuretic. More on that later.

Dandelion greens are best in early spring before they are done flowering. Harvesting late in the season is kind of like picking lettuce and spinach after they have bolted—edible, but not at their best. If you had a few dandelions take root in your garden last year, they are probably ready to uproot and eat right now. Sort of a new twist on the phrase "weed-and-feed."

Young greens can be blanched and served in salad, or else boiled, but I like them best when chopped and sautéed. They go well in omelets, stir-fry, soup, casserole, or any savory dish for that matter. Fresh roots can be peeled, thinly sliced and sautéed. A real treat is dandelion crowns. The reason they flower so early is that they have fully-formed flower bud clusters tucked into the center of the root crown, whereas many other flowers bloom on new growth. After cutting off the leaves, take a paring knife and excise the crowns, which can be steamed and served with butter.

Roasted dandelion roots make the best coffee substitute I have ever tasted, and that's saying something because I really love coffee. Scrub fresh roots and spread them out on an oven rack so they are not touching each other. You can experiment with higher settings, but I roast them at about 250 until they are crispy and dark brown throughout. Honestly I can't say just how long it takes, somewhere between 2 and 3 hours. At any rate I always roast them when I have to be in the house anyway, and check them frequently after the two-hour mark. Grind them using a food processor or mortar and pestle. Compared to coffee, you use a bit less of the ground root per cup.

The beverage tastes dandy, but as mentioned above, it is more diuretic than coffee or black tea. I have never found this a problem, but if your morning commute frequently involves a traffic snarl, choose your breakfast drink accordingly.

I have not tried dandelion wine, a tradition that dates back centuries in Europe, and so have no first-hand experience to report, but scads of recipes can be found on the Internet. Several friends and family members have tried it, with negative and positive reviews pretty well split. I have no idea if it is personal preference or wine-making skill that is so evenly divided.

Given all the virtues of dandelions, it is amazing how much time and treasure our culture puts into eradicating them. It seems to verge on an obsession with some people, who drench their lawn with selective broadleaf herbicides like 2,4-D, dicamba and mecoprop. These all come with health risks, not to mention hefty price tags.

For those who perhaps take the whole lion connection too far and can't sleep at night if there are dandelions lurking on the premises, I'll share a secret to getting them out of the landscape. Setting the mower to cut at four inches high will not only get rid of most weeds, it will help prevent diseases, and will greatly reduce the need for fertilizer.

I say we stop trying to kill the only North American lion that is not in danger of extinction, and learn to appreciate and use it more.

A Tale of Nine Lives

The two cats at my place have survived many life-threatening traumas such as falls, fights and even the compulsory "devotions" of small children. It's amazing the hazards they can weather. I find it disappointing that experts in the veterinary field continue to assert cats have but a single life, and that the whole nine-lives thing is just a cat tale.

However, the story about cattails having (at least) nine lives is no yarn. An obligate wetland plant, the common cattail (*Typha*

116

latifolia) is native to the Americas as well as to Europe, Africa and most of Asia—basically the planet minus Australia, all Pacific Islands and most Polar regions. It can be found growing along wetland margins and into water up to 30 inches deep, from hot climates to Canada's Yukon Territory.

Its name comes from the brown puffy seed head it produces which resembles, um, well really a corn dog. But to avoid an epidemic of incessant laughter, the authorities went with cattail.

Aptly named or not, the cattail is truly a wonder of nature. As

someone who likes to eat more than three meals a day, it makes sense that I first got acquainted with the culinary uses of cattails. The young shoots, sometimes called Cossack asparagus, are delicious raw or cooked (definitely opt for cooking them if you're unsure of the water purity).

The thick rhizomes (tuber-like roots) are about 80% carbohydrates and between 3% and 8% protein, better than some cultivated crops. Rhizomes can be baked, boiled, or dried and ground into flour. In his book *Stalking the Wild Asparagus*, Euell Gibbons details how to process roots with water to extract starch, which I'd have to say works nicely. The starch, wet or powdered, is added to flour to enhance the nutrient value of foods like biscuits and pancakes.

What I like best are the flower spikes, which are two-tiered

117

affairs with the male (staminate) pollen-bearing spikes on top and the thicker female (pistillate) heads below. The male flower spikes wither away after they do their thing, but the female spikes mature into the corn dogs—I mean cats' tails—we all recognize. Both spikes are edible, but must be gathered just as they break out of their papery sheaths. Boil and eat with butter as you would corn on the cob. They taste just like chicken. Kidding—they're similar to corn.

In the fall you can gather the tails and burn off the fluff to harvest the edible, oil-rich seeds. (Confession: due to my undiagnosed Laziness Syndrome I haven't yet tried this.)

For years, I and my daughter sally forth (not her real name) in mid- to late June and gather bright yellow cattail pollen. Just slip a plastic bag over the flower head, shake a few times and you're done. An acre of cattails can yield over three tons of cattail pollen, and at 6-7% protein, that's a lot of nutritious flour. Substitute cattail pollen for up to one-fourth of the flour in any recipe. You can use more, but experiment on a small scale before you serve it to others (a tip from my kids).

OK, we're up to five lives, I think. Euell Gibbons called cattail the supermarket of the swamp, and he wasn't kidding. You can find thousands of articles and research papers on the uses of cattails. Technically that might not get us to nine lives yet, so let's name some names.

Native peoples around the world (except as noted) wove cattail leaves and flower stalks into roof thatch, sleeping mats, duck decoys, hats, dolls and other kids' toys, to name but a few uses. Fresh leaves and roots were pounded and used as poultices on boils. Cattail fluff was used as diaper linings, moccasin insulation and wound dressings.

118

Today cattail swamps are created by engineers for treating wastewater, and artisans make paper from cattail leaves. And kids still have fun playing with the leaves and especially the mature cats' tails. Here's to the many lives of the cattail. But let's try and change its name to the corn-dog tail. The world could use the extra laughter.

Eye Candy and Cough Syrup

I haven't checked with an optometrist, but I may have a winter-related vision problem. When five or six months of winter-white finally give way to a mostly brown world each early spring, my eyeballs hurt—they ache for something bright in the landscape. That's probably why I plant a few additional crocus bulbs in the yard every fall, and why I search wooded areas for early-blooming native wildflowers like bloodroot and Carolina spring beauty.

But what thrills me most is how clumps of bright yellow coltsfoot flowers emerge, long before their leaves come out, from muddy

roadside ditches, rail embankments and other places with a history of soil disturbance. Coltsfoot is native to Europe and Asia, but has naturalized throughout North America. Its flowers look like small dandelions, but with no leaves to go with them. Maybe it's the contrast between their color and the sepia environs, or perhaps it's their audacity at blooming so early, but these little sunbursts go a long way toward dispelling my winter eye fatigue.

Many non-native plants came here accidentally, but coltsfoot was likely planted by early settlers because of its history as a medicinal plant. We don't know if coltsfoot cheered up European settlers when the snow melted, but we do know that they used it to treat coughs and colds during winter's icy grip.

Its botanical genus name is *Tussilago*, derived from the Latin word for cough. Its common name comes from the fact that its leaves, which emerge as the flowers die back, have a shape similar to a horse's hoof.

Pliny the Elder (think Socrates, but Roman instead of Greek and slightly less ancient) treated his asthma by inhaling the smoke of dried coltsfoot leaves and flowers. In an ironic and tragic twist, Pliny died of smoke inhalation during the eruption of Mount Vesuvius.

There was a period of time in Europe when the coltsfoot blossom was the symbol for an apothecary, sort of an old-time drugstore that dispenses herbal medicine. Back in the day, those yellow flowers were virtually synonymous with healing. And following a tradition that dates back thousands of years, some Chinese today still use commercial cough syrups made with coltsfoot.

Just because something is all-natural doesn't mean it's all-benign. The truth is that herbal remedies are nothing to sneeze at. Consider digitalis, quinine and THC, potent drugs that come from plants. Because the active ingredients in herbal medicine can interact with prescription medications or exacerbate health conditions, no herbal remedy should ever be used without first consulting a licensed medical professional.

In fact there is concern about the safety of coltsfoot in some quarters. In a 1999 University of Iowa study, researchers documented an increase in liver cancer among rats ingesting large doses of coltsfoot. However, because the Iowa study concluded coltsfoot's health risk was due to one particular compound that it (the plant, not the study) contained, some German researchers are working to develop a coltsfoot strain that's free of the chemical.

Making coltsfoot into cough syrup requires supervision, but using it as a tonic for the spirit need not involve doctors. I encourage everyone to check out these splashy early-blooming flowers. You can't overdose on eye candy.

Nettles

One of my favorite plants is either highly versatile, or very confused. On the one hand, professional herbivores like rabbits and deer refuse to even touch it, but many people, myself included, will gladly eat it every day it is available. While contacting it is painful, it has been proven to relieve certain chronic pain. It is steeped in over a thousand years of folklore, at one point imbued with the power to cleanse away sin, yet medical science recognizes it as a legitimate remedy for many disorders. Some gardeners consider it a bothersome weed, but others actually cultivate it.

The stinging nettle, *Urtica dioica,* is native to Europe, Asia, and northern Africa but has been widespread throughout North America from northern Mexico to northern Canada for centuries.

Experts disagree as to the number of nettle species and subspecies worldwide. To confuse matters, many of these cross with one another to form hybrids. Although a few species do not sting, if it's nettle and it gives you a rash, it's fair to call it stinging nettle.

Nettles sprout little hypodermic needles on stems, leaves, and even their flowers. Called trichomes, these glass-like silica-based needles inject a mixture of irritating chemicals upon contact. The

cocktail varies by species, but usually includes histamine, 5-HTP, serotonin, formic acid and acetylcholine.

So why would one place this well-armed adversary in their mouth? Well, when nettles are cooked, the stinging hairs are destroyed. Furthermore, nettles are the tastiest cooked green—wild or domestic—that I have ever had. It tastes a lot like spinach, except sweeter. Nettles can be boiled, steamed, or stir-fried. They are great by themselves or in soups, omelets, pesto, casseroles, or pretty much any savory dish you can come up with.

One of the things I really like about nettles is that they are some of the first green things to get going after the snow melts. I should mention that only the tops of young plants are harvested to eat. The good thing is that the more you pick, the more young tops grow back. Eventually they will get too tall and tough, but frequent picking can stretch nettle season well into June.

On a dry-weight basis, nettles are higher in protein—about 15% —than almost any other leafy green vegetable. They are a good source of iron, potassium, calcium, and Vitamins A and C, and have a healthy ratio of Omega-3 to Omega-6 fatty acids. Because drying also neutralizes nettles' sting, they have been used as fodder for domestic animals. Today nettles are commonly fed to laying hens to improve their productivity.

The University of Maryland Medical Center reports that nettles can help relieve symptoms, such as difficulty urinating, of Benign Prostatic Hyperplasia (BPH) in men. In terms of using pain to relieve pain, the U of M Medical Center also states that research "...suggests that some people find relief from joint pain by applying nettle leaf topically to the painful area. Other studies show that taking an oral extract of stinging nettle, along with nonsteroidal anti-inflammatory drugs (NSAIDs), allowed people to reduce their NSAID dose."

As *The Cat in the Hat* said, that is not all. You'd think the U of M was selling nettles the way they seem to promote them. Consider this endorsement:

> "One preliminary human study suggested that nettle capsules helped reduce sneezing and itching in people with hay fever. In another study, 57% of patients rated nettles as effective in relieving allergies, and 48% said that nettles were more effective than allergy medications they had used previously."

Gardeners use nettles as a "green manure" because they (nettles, that is—gardeners may be nitrogen-rich, but they're not routinely added to soil.) are high in nitrogen, as well as iron and manganese. Nettles can also help attract beneficial insects.

What can't you do with nettles? I guess they're kind of like Dr. Seuss' "thneed." Turns out you can wear them, too. Nettles have been used for 2,000 years as a source of fiber for cloth-making. During World War I, Germany used nettle fiber to make military uniforms. I have made cordage from nettle stems using a simple technique called reverse-wrapping.

If you have a nettle patch, put away the weed killer, and consider yourself lucky.

First Blooms

One of the earliest woody plants to blossom is the juneberry. It is either a small tree or a shrub, depending on who you ask, which makes me wonder if it's hiding something. In fact, this thing has more aliases than one of America's Most Wanted. Variously known as serviceberry, shadbush, shadwood, shadblow, Saskatoon, juneberry and wild-plum, the small-to-medium size tree also answers to *Amelanchier canadensis*, its botanical name. Of those options, I prefer juneberry even though its fruit may ripen in early July in northern New York State.

It's the first native woody plant to produce conspicuous flowers, and its white blossoms can be seen on roadsides, in fencerows and on forest edges before most trees push out any leaves. The smooth, gray-silver bark is attractive in its own right. Depending on conditions, juneberries may grow as a multi-stem clump, but more often develop as single-trunk trees reaching 25 to 40 feet tall. Not only are its early blossoms an aesthetic treat, they're advertising the location of a source of berries that boast more nutrient value than almost any other native fruit.

Juneberries are often overlooked as a food source, partly because birds may beat us to the punch, and partly because juneberries grow tall enough that the fruit is sometimes out of reach. Because juneberries have less moisture than blueberries, they're slightly higher in protein and carbohydrates, making them a great food for athletes and other active people.

The soft, dark purple berries have twice as much potassium and iron as blueberries in addition to large amounts of magnesium and phosphorous. Juneberries also have plenty of vitamin C, thiamin, riboflavin, pantothenic acid, vitamin B-6, vitamin A and vitamin E.

Juneberries make an attractive landscape plant, and can be used to entice songbirds like cedar waxwings to your yard. *Amelanchier alnifolia*, a species from the Northern Plains closely related to our northeastern *A. canadensis*, is better for home use, as it does not grow as tall, so the fruit will always be within reach. It can tolerate a wide range of site conditions and will thrive even in poor soils. Full sun is a must, however. Another plus is that juneberry foliage turns a remarkable salmon-pink in the fall, adding to its value as a landscape shrub.

The berries are delectable fresh, and make excellent pies. They're especially good for freezing, as they make excellent, nutrient-packed smoothies year-round. It's helpful to freeze them first on cookie sheets, and then transfer them to bulk containers. That way they don't form the kind of monolithic juneberry glacier that requires a chisel, adult supervision and a first-aid kit to break off a chunk.

Native peoples across northern North America valued juneberries, and European settlers followed their example. You too can take advantage of this under-appreciated wild fruit. This is a great time to make note of the location of juneberry plants for harvesting this summer. For more juicy juneberry tidbits, visit www.juneberries.org.

Goldenrod

Late summer brings us an amazing array of wildflowers. First the ragged, pale-blue chicory blossoms appear alongside the stately white umbels of Queen-Anne's lace, gracing roadways and pastures. These are followed by the  tall, lavender Joe-Pye weed in low-lying areas, and finally we become awash in brilliant oceans of mustard-yellow goldenrod blooms.

At the same time, hay fever symptoms are ramping up. As goldenrod becomes the dominant wildflower on the scene, an increased pollen load in the air makes life miserable for those who suffer from allergies. Because of this correlation, it seems logical to blame goldenrod for one's red itchy eyes, sinus congestion, sneezing, and general histamine-soaked misery.

But there is an easy way to tell for sure if the gilded weed is to blame, a one-question test: Have you noticed a lot of bees up your nose recently? If yes, then goldenrod might be guilty. If no, there is another culprit lurking about.

While most plants respond to late summer's shorter days by starting to wind down their business for the season, goldenrod is a "short-day" plant, the sort that is stimulated to bloom by waning day length. It's a perennial in the aster family, and is widespread across North America. We have something on the order of 130 species of goldenrod in the genus *Solidago*.

As one of the most abundant blooms of late summer and early autumn, this native wildflower is for many insects, including numerous bee species, a vital source of nectar as well as nutritious pollen. Unfortunately, this latter item has given goldenrod a black eye among many allergy sufferers.

Though goldenrod's showy yellow flowers are in full view on roadsides and in meadows and pastures, it can't be guilty because its pollen is very heavy. That's a relative term, I suppose, since it is light enough for bees to carry it around. But in the pollen realm it's heavy—and is also sticky—and it is not able to be blown far from the plant. It's not that goldenrod pollen would not trigger an allergic response, it's just that for such a thing to happen, someone or something would have to deposit its pollen directly into your schnozz. And in general, bees are not in the habit of doing so.

Not only is goldenrod guiltless of allergic assault, it has been used as an alternate source of rubber. Henry Ford was intrigued by the potential uses of goldenrod, and reportedly made some tires based on the plant in the 1930s. Interest in goldenrod was revived during World War II. Goldenrod is also used in herbal medicine to help treat kidney stones, sore throats and toothaches.

So who's to blame for the spike in late summer allergies? Surprisingly, the culprit is goldenrod's cousin, ragweed, although it doesn't behave at all like its golden relative (I suspect we all have a relative or two like this in our family tree). Ragweed, another native plant, is also in the aster family, but unlike goldenrod it churns out loads of very light pollen.

Just how light is it? Ragweed pollen can remain airborne for several days, and significant quantities have been found as far as 400 miles out to sea. And a single ragweed plant can produce a billion pollen grains to fly on the breeze and make you sneeze. Yep, this is the stuff that stuffs you up.

One reason we don't suspect ragweed is that its blossoms are dull green and look nothing like a typical flower. It's as if they're trying not to attract attention. You can almost imagine them thinking, "heh, heh—let goldenrod take the rap." The reason ragweed is inconspicuous is that it's wind-pollinated and has no need to "advertise" with bright colors and sweet nectar to entice pollinators. Turns out it's way easier to attract wind than bees.

Most ragweed species—there are about 50 of them—are annual, but they come back year after year from the copious seeds they produce each fall. Ragweed will keep billowing allergens until the first hard frost, so let's hope it's not too much of an extended season this year. And let's try to spread the word about goldenrod to spare it any further false accusations.

Not Just for Breakfast Any More

"Never eat anything bigger than your head." I don't know if cartoonist Bernard Kliban came up with that or if it's a nugget of old folk wisdom. Certainly you should not eat anything that big without at least chewing it first. But if you like mushrooms, you can find wild ones that are in fact much larger than your head.

The giant puffball, *Calvatia gigantea*, appears in late summer and early fall in pastures, lawns and deciduous forests. These brilliant white globes are the fruiting bodies of the actual fungus, which is out of sight below ground. They seem to magically appear overnight, and are typically six to twenty inches in diameter. In rare instances they have reached nearly five feet across, bigger than the heads of all but the most conceited individuals.

To be sure, fresh puffballs are inflated and puffy, but their name comes from what happens once they mature and dry out. In that condition, a smoke-like stream of brown spores will jet from the top of a dry puffball any time it is disturbed. A puffball may produce as many as 7,000,000,000,000 spores, so it can puff seemingly forever. Back in "the day" kids used to think it was a riot to step on these. More than likely, there's now a cell phone app that is more convenient, and hypoallergenic.

Statistically speaking, most wild mushrooms are edible. A few,

129

though, cause irreversible liver failure; hence it is a drag to mess up. In addition to these deadly *Amanita* species there are other types which cause gastric discomfort (some spectacularly), all the more reason to be careful. I know a couple of self-taught mushroom hunters with decades of experience who in rare cases still make a mistake. Even morels and chanterelles, considered easy to find, have dangerous look-alike species. Fortunately for the well-being of the public I readily admit mushroom identification is not one of my strong suits, and I'm usually reluctant to make a positive ID on a specimen.

One of the few exceptions is the easily recognized giant puffball. I suppose a determined soul might be able to get it wrong, but it would take some real talent at screwing up. If you follow a few simple rules it is nearly impossible to mistake a giant puffball for anything else:

Small is bad. Remember where "giant" is part of its name? The problem is, a toxic *Amanita* mushroom when newly-emerging, before its cap unfolds, can resemble an undersized puffball. So only select ones six inches in diameter or bigger.

Perhaps the only place where white is best is where puffballs, tennis attire and office paper are concerned. Cut open your giant puffball. If its flesh is white as the driven, pre-Industrial Age snow, it's good. Slight yellowing indicates it has become too mature. Eating it at this stage is not dangerous but it won't taste as good and might give you a belly ache.

"Homogenous is next to Godliness," as they say. Actually no one says that, but when you slice a puffball its interior should look uniform. Any hint of an outline of a stem, gills or still-folded cap means it's dangerous. Back away slowly in case it tries any sudden moves.

However, if your find is large, and white with no "shadow" or outline inside, it is almost certainly the real deal. If it's your first time as a wild mycophage, though, check with someone (preferably one with knowledge in this area) before serving it for supper.

No one claims puffballs are as delectable as a morel, but I think they are on par with a grocery-store mushroom. They can be cut into strips and sautéed just like commercial mushrooms. Puffballs can also be sliced and frozen for later, which is great in light of that head-size restriction mentioned earlier.

My father used to relate how, when he was little, his mother pan-fried large thin puffball slices and served them with maple syrup like pancakes. "Heavenly," was how he described them. One day he finally tried to recreate this delicacy. We both agreed that puffballs with maple syrup fell a few steps short of Nirvana. Much better in sauce or a stir-fry, I think.

Milkweed

After the cloud-flocks of blackbirds have departed, swarming in their amoeba-like fashion toward points south, and the broad chevrons of geese have mostly disappeared over the horizon, another momentous fall event begins. Yes, it's time for one more native species to take to the air—the great milkweed migration is on.

By late summer, milkweed pods are bursting with mature seeds affixed to bundles of platinum floss that lie damp and orderly, waiting for autumn emancipation. Following a good frost each pod dries out and splits perfectly along a seam into two boat-like halves, exposing a cache of silk. The wind teases this material

131

from the dry-docked pod halves, launching countless puffy, seed-bearing paratroopers to the wind.

Many farmers and gardeners are not impressed by such choreography, as milkweed can be a real nuisance in some crops.

Not only is it a perennial, it spreads quite effectively through its robust root system as well as its migratory seeds. However, certain butterflies are happy about the white parachutes of autumn.

The survival of North American monarch butterflies (worldwide, they are in no danger) depends on continual access to milkweed from their winter home in Mexico up to the Great Lakes as they move northward each spring. Recently monarch populations have declined sharply, due in large part to habitat loss in Mexico, but also to milkweed issues. Increased use of agricultural herbicides along with continued urban sprawl have resulted in less milkweed. In addition, monarch caterpillars are being poisoned when insecticide-tainted corn pollen drifts onto the milkweed plants they're eating.

Farmers and butterflies may soon be playing for the same team, though, because milkweed is poised to become an economically viable crop. Native peoples and settlers used milkweed for food, medicine, fiber and even sugar, and we've all heard how its buoyant floss was gathered during World War II and used by the military in life preservers.

But modern research is what has landed our native, latex-bearing "weed" on the economic map. The Agricultural Research Service, a division of the United States Department of Agriculture, has found a number of important new uses for milkweed.

The silky floss is already in use in the textile industry. Companies like the Natural Fibers Corporation of Ogallala, NE use it in comforters and down jackets. One of the main advantages of milkweed floss compared to goose down is that it is hypo-allergenic. It's also 10% warmer, 20% more durable and 50% more breathable than down. As an added plus, it appeals to consumers who don't want goods made with animal products. During WWII, schoolchildren gathered floss by hand for life jackets, but today it can be harvested on a large scale with a slightly modified grain combine.

One of the byproducts of floss production is milkweed seed, which is can't be fed to livestock because it's poisonous. Research done in Illinois and Washington State found a silver lining—its toxicity makes it valuable as a pesticide against fall armyworms and certain nematodes, which can devastate alfalfa, soybeans, potatoes and many other crops. In one trial, ground milkweed seed, tilled into the soil, killed 97% of destructive nematodes.

The fact that milkweed sap, or latex, is rich in hydrocarbons has been known for decades. Funding from the United States Department of Energy enabled a private Utah-based research firm called Native Plants (subsequently financed by an oil company) to start investigating latex as a source of crude oil.

Before it flowers, milkweed is mowed and baled using

conventional farm equipment, and then processed to extract oil. The residue, which is 20% protein, can be used as animal feed. Although at current prices it is not profitable to extract oil from milkweed, that could easily change in the future.

But more work is needed before milkweed hits the mainstream. It turns out that while patches of milkweed thrive on roadsides and in meadows, when it is grown on a large scale as a monoculture, disease becomes a problem.

And then there's the question of milkweed's image. According to the founder and CEO of Natural Fibers Corporation, one of his marketing obstacles is that "weed" is in the title. Dropping it is out of the question, as the Dairy Council tells me that the name "milk" is already taken.

Cranberries

Like the political process, cranberries can leave a sour taste in your mouth. But unlike politics, whose bitter aftertaste cuts through any amount of sweetener, the flavor of cranberries is readily improved with a little sugar.

To say a fresh cranberry is sour is like saying Paris is a nice town. In fact, it (the berry, not Paris) can have a lower pH value than stomach acid. It's almost a wonder people ever started eating them.

The cranberry, which is closely related to blueberries, is native to higher latitudes of the northern hemisphere the world over. It is an evergreen trailing vine, or sometimes a very small shrub. The name is derived from its flower petals, which are reflexed or pulled back sharply, making its pink blossom resemble (to some) the head and bill of a crane. The North American species is *Vaccinium macrocarpon*, and luckily for us it has larger berries than species in northern Europe and elsewhere.

It's important to note that the shrub known as highbush cranberry is an imposter and is not related to the stuff we eat on Thanksgiving. This kind of confusion around common names happens a lot. In the plant world there are no copyright laws, which is why pointy-headed plant nerds like yours truly like those fancy Latin names.

Of course we know that Native Americans made use of cranberries, and introduced them to early European immigrants. A firsthand account from the late 1500s describes how some Algonquins brought cups full of cranberries to newly arrived Pilgrims as they came ashore. I'm thinking that unless there was a bit of maple sugar in with the berries, maybe their purpose was actually to discourage the migrants from staying.

The colonists took a shine to the little red sourballs occasionally known as moss berries or bear berries, and by the 1820s some farmers began exporting this new crop back to Europe. Growing them might not look like you'd expect, though—images of cranberries floating on what appears to be a lake give the wrong impression.

Wild cranberries are often found in wet areas such as bogs, but cultivated berries are grown on carefully managed upland fields. These sandy plots, laser-leveled and heavily irrigated, are surrounded by berms so the fields can be flooded with six to eight inches of water to make harvesting easier. Because berries gathered this way have a very short shelf life, they are generally frozen, canned or otherwise processed right away. Cranberries for fresh eating are usually hand-picked in dry fields.

Over the past few decades, cranberries have been touted for an increasingly wide range of health benefits as well as for their taste. It has long been known they are high in Vitamins C and E, pantothenic acid, as well as manganese, copper and other minerals. But it's their antioxidant properties that have gotten people excited.

If you saw "oligomeric proanthocyanidins" listed on a candy bar you might not buy it. But these and many other natural compounds are abundant in cranberries, and despite the scary names they're good for you. Cranberries are being intensively studied for potential benefits in treating diabetes, arthritis, cancer and other illnesses.

Research suggests cranberry juice—the good stuff, not the corn syrup-laden wannabe juice—may help prevent calcium-based kidney stones. Moderation in all things, as too much of it may cause oxalic acid-based bladder stones.

Studies also indicate cranberry juice does prevent certain harmful bacteria from sticking to us. Turns out it's like Teflon for them. While cranberry juice has not been found effective for treating urinary tract infections, it is good at preventing them by stopping coliform bacteria from adhering to places they don't belong. Good news for your teeth, too—cranberries help keep decay microbes from glomming on to enamel, thus reducing dental plaque and cavities.

If political news gets you down, you'll be happy to hear that cranberries also help prevent ulcer-causing bacteria from colonizing human stomach lining and forming ulcers. Furthermore, their cardiovascular benefits include lowering "bad" LDL cholesterol blood levels and increasing those of the good HDL cholesterol. So if you're a news junkie, keep the cranberries close at hand during broadcasts.

A Sight for Sore Eyes and Other Ailments

As summer wanes, our local pharmacy really stocks up on inventory. You might say it comes into full bloom. Just to clarify, that's not a business report, it's a botanical one. I have no idea how the drugstore industry is faring, but three of our most versatile and storied medicinal herbs begin flowering in late summer, and they're a sight to behold.

The three show-off healing plants are: purple-flowering Joe-Pye weed, the doctor; his nurse boneset with her crisp white cap, and their immigrant neighbor, valerian, also bearing white. One of the reasons they're a visual treat is that they often grow in vast swaths in wet areas. Sometimes they co-mingle, and other times you'll drive past an undulating wave of purple Joe-Pye weed, followed by one of white boneset. I suggest doing an image search of these plants so you'll know what to look for.

Tradition has it that Joe Pye was a Native American who used this plant to heal New Englanders of typhus. The plant was officially recognized by the medical community as a medicine in the 1800s, and is still well respected today for its effectiveness. Its roots are used to treat a number of ailments, especially kidney and bladder stones, and for this reason, some know it as gravel root.

"Nurse" boneset is a native plant, like her close relative to Joe-Pye weed, and is no less important as a medicinal herb. Though never sanctioned as a legitimate drug, boneset, which I always think of as *Eupatorium perfoliatum* (true story, sadly) was reportedly used widely in the 18th and 19th centuries. It was taken to reduce fever and congestion, and even today some people drink tea made from its leaves when they have a cold or the flu.

Valerian root, a common ingredient in herbal supplements intended to help relieve anxiety and sleeplessness, has been used throughout Europe and Asia for at least a thousand years. It's seldom sold as a bulk herb, though, because of its smell. Some compare its odor to stale perspiration, but I think that's an unfair claim. It's much worse than that. Valerian is very powerful, and should be taken with caution, and never on a long-term basis.

While medicinal herbs can be beneficial, it's essential to check with your doctor before taking any, and to only use them under the supervision of an experienced herbalist. Medicinal plants are exactly that, medicine, some much stronger than others. They have the potential to react with prescription drugs, and in rare cases can aggravate conditions such as glaucoma.

Whether or not you ever make use of these medicinal plants, they put on a show in August and September, and I hope you get to enjoy the performance.

Aliens in the Landscape

Imagine if you ventured out on a rainy afternoon and found a bright yellow slime-blob slithering across your perennial gardens, one that had not been there the previous day. Let's say this amoeba-like thing was growing larger by the minute as it dissolved and consumed organic matter it encountered on its way through your yard. You might look around for Steve McQueen and the rest of the cast of the 1958 classic horror film "The Blob," right? Just before you called 911.

While it sounds like fiction, this scenario does happen (minus Steve McQueen et al.) during periods of wet weather on mulched beds, in the woods, and other places with abundant organic matter. Of course, there are some key qualifications to the above description. The blob, called a plasmodial slime mold, is slimy, though not a mold. What it is, precisely, is still up for debate.

Fortunately, this freak of nature moves slowly—a foot per day at most—and there is an upper limit to its size, maybe twenty inches across. Also it engulfs things like bacteria and rotting vegetation—you need not worry about pets and small children near a slime mold.

It is a tired cliché that things were simpler in the past, but in some ways it's true. When I was a kid you had three television stations, one kind of phone and only two options when you ordered coffee. I don't claim it was better, but it was simpler for sure.

And in the great outdoors if you found some living thing you didn't recognize, there were three possibilities—it was either an animal, plant, or fungus. Animals were relatively big and could move around, plants did not travel and were usually green, and fungi grew on decaying wood and behaved themselves. Single-celled organisms didn't really count because you couldn't see them. It's not that simple today.

In high school we learned about the five divisions of living things, three of which were microbial. Soon after, it got switched to three domains, and now the powers-that-be (whoever they are) tell us there are six kingdoms of life-forms. Undoubtedly this will change again next week, so don't fret about it.

As their category-waffling suggests, taxonomists argue a lot. Over the years, the plasmodial slime mold has given them much to provoke disagreements. A single-cell organism, a slime mold may live its entire life as a solitary and immobile microbe. But if conditions are right it will start to form a plasmodium, gliding across the landscape and engulfing other slime-mold cells in addition to organic matter, and growing to pancake-size. It does this while remaining a single cell, albeit one with millions of free-floating nuclei from all the hapless slime mold organisms it ate.

Long considered fungi, slime molds are now lumped in with protists, a category which is more or less the "island of misfits" for microbes. Protists are a varied lot—some are pathogens that cause malaria, sleeping sickness, giardiasis, and other nasty illnesses, while some are innocuous, for example algae and slime mold.

Ranging in color from brown, white, or blue-gray to brilliant yellow, slime molds have been mistaken for dog vomit, and in some places are known as demon puke. Not exactly endearing, but they do help recycle nutrients in the environment. And it's not their fault they're so common.

Here in the Northeast we now get something like three inches more precipitation than we did forty years ago. In addition, our "new normal" weather patterns include long blocks of wet. Sadly, these conditions are ideal for plant pathogens, but they also favor slime molds, which you are as likely to see growing on wood-chip mulch in suburbia as in the forest.

Like some of us, the 1958 Blob was rendered inert by extreme cold. In the movie it was airlifted to the far north where, as the protagonist explained, it will no longer be a threat to humans, "...as long as the Arctic stays cold."

Uh-oh. Maybe we should start carrying ice packs, just in case.

Vengeful Veggies

It's not unheard of for people to burn vegetables now and then, especially if you're as easily distracted as I am. I'll think, the potatoes need a few more minutes, so there's plenty of time to run out to the garden for chives. Thirty minutes later I'll be weeding the sweet corn patch, sans chives, when the smoke alarm indicates the potatoes are "done." Oops.

While it seems absurd to think that vegetables might burn us, it does happen, and the latter half of summer is peak season for it. The burn is chemical in nature, and the vegetable is wild parsnip, an invasive species whose population has exploded in recent years.

Related to Queen Anne's lace, wild parsnip grows three to six feet tall, and is topped by yellow "umbrellas" of flowers which bloom any time from late June through July. Wild parsnip can be found in vacant lots as well as in yards and gardens. But because it has been so effectively spread by mowing equipment, mile after mile of it can be seen along roadsides throughout the Northeast.

The root of wild parsnip is in fact edible, same as the parsnips we grow in our gardens. However, the sap contained in its leaves and stems, like the sap of giant hogweed, is phytophototoxic. The only good thing about this word is that it may help you in a Scrabble game. It means wild parsnip sap on your skin reacts

142

with sunlight to damage proteins and cause severe burns. And by severe I mean burns that take months or sometimes years to heal, and the scars may be permanent. The sap can even cause blindness if it gets in your eyes.

It seems fair to ask why garden-variety parsnips do not burn people. They can, but we do not let them. Like all root crops, parsnips are biennial. In their first year they develop a robust root, which they would normally use for energy to make a tall flower stalk the second year. But we thwart their desire for offspring by harvesting them at the end of the first season (which could be their source of resentment). By harvest time, parsnip leaves are generally yellow and faded, if present at all. No green leaves, no sap, no burns.

It's a small consolation, but you will not get burned by merely brushing up against this plant, and once it is dry it poses no threat, unlike the case with poison ivy. All the same, it's probably a good idea to wear gloves and long sleeves when handling wild parsnip. If you do get sap on your skin, get indoors (out of the sun) as soon as possible and wash with soap and water.

As everyone knows, when facing a zombie apocalypse, you grab a shovel and aim for their heads. Shovels are also useful in battling the parsnip-ocalypse we now face, except you aim for their feet. Wild parsnips have taproots which are very hard to pull out, but which are easily cut with a shovel. You don't have to get the whole root; just dig as deep as you can to sever the taproot, pry the plant up and it will die. You don't even have to touch the thing.

If you're hopelessly outnumbered by wild parsnips, at least mow them to prevent them from making seeds while you muster a posse of shovel-wielding townsfolk (pitchforks and torches are

143

optional) to help you. But do wear protective clothing and safety glasses when mowing wild parsnip, and unless you have a Level-A Hazmat suit, do not use a string trimmer on it.

Glyphosate, the active ingredient in herbicides like Roundup, works on wild parsnip. Herbicide is most effective when used on first-year plants, called rosettes, which are the ones without a flower stalk. The best time to spray is in late summer or early fall. Treating early in the season may kill the top, but often the root will live to send up another flower spike.

I distinctly remember having scorched some parsnips years ago, so I hope none of this is some kind of revenge. Please try not to burn any more vegetables, lest they all become vengeful.

Caterpillar Eats Dog Strangler

Sometimes called "dog-strangling vine," swallow-wort doesn't harm pets, but it does live up to its name as a strangler. There are two species of the perennial vine, both adept at choking out wildflowers, forest seedlings, hay fields and other habitats. In the Eastern Lake Ontario region, this invasive plant from Eurasia has proved capable of blanketing large tracts, hundreds of acres in some cases, to create permanent monocultures of tangled, toxic foliage.

While there are subtle differences between pale and black swallow-wort, they behave alike, and it makes sense to treat them as one. Heck, botanists are still fighting about whether swallow-worts are in the genus *Cynanchum* or *Vincetoxicum*, so let's consider them the same.

Swallow-wort has so many vile tricks up its proverbial sleeve, I think even Emperor Palpatine from *Star Wars* would be jealous. It can grow in nearly all soil types, has a robust, Medusa-like root system which poisons competing vegetation, and it is endowed with super-powers where seed production is concerned.

Related to the common milkweed, swallow-wort attracts monarch butterflies, which lay eggs on it. The problem there is that the caterpillars die from eating the toxic leaves. In fact, the vine is so noxious that nothing, not even insects, feed on it. Amazingly, it can bounce back from powerful herbicides like glyphosate (the active ingredient in products such as Roundup), apparently stronger than ever. No wonder biologists and agronomists have been losing sleep over it.

So it's with much relief that a new hope has appeared. While dog-strangling vine has withstood mowers, rototillers, flame throwers (true) and potent agrochemicals, it's no match for this brute, which was identified by researchers from the University of Rhode Island and others in 2013. At roughly a tenth of the weight of a paper clip and a fraction of an inch long, our hero is a caterpillar, *Hypena opulenta*, the larva of a Ukrainian moth.

In its native range, swallow-wort is a well-behaved plant because the tiny *Hypena opulenta* caterpillar, along with other insects, keep it in check. In fact, Carleton University biologist Naomi Cappuccino, a Canadian researcher who went to Ukraine with

145

URI scientists to look for biological controls, said they had a hard time locating swallow-wort; it was that scarce.

Finding biological controls for exotic invasive plants is no easy task, and requires traveling to the plant's home environment to make field observations in all kinds of conditions. But once an insect, pathogen or vertebrate is identified, the real work begins. Years of quarantine with carefully controlled trials are needed to be sure a potential hero won't end up going over to the Dark Side when swallow-wort gets scarce, eating corn and soybeans or something like that. In the past, "miracle cure" controls have done more harm than good (e.g. the cane toad in Australia and the mongoose in Hawaii), so a great deal of care is taken to approve biocontrols today.

In Canada, *Hypena opulenta* was released in 2013, and it is already putting a dent in the dog-strangler population in some places. The hope is that we will eventually have a success story like we have had with purple loosestrife, which was poised to wreak great harm to freshwater wetland ecosystems before biocontrols were introduced. Even if *Hypena opulenta* performs admirably, it may be a while before we notice much difference. To paraphrase Princess Leia, "Help us, *Hypena opulenta*; you're our only hope." Thus far, at least.

Doddering

Considering the climate where the personification of evil is alleged to make his home, you'd think the devil would wear flip-flops or sandals, but it seems he prefers lace-up footwear (Prada, I'm told). "Devil's shoelaces" is one name applied to dodder (*Cuscuta spp.*), a parasitic plant that looks more like creepy yellow-orange spaghetti than a plant. Dodder is known by a whole slew of unflattering titles including wizard's net, strangleweed, witch's hair, and hellbine. As these names suggest, dodder has earned itself quite a sinister reputation, which is no big surprise, since parasites generally inspire collywobbles, not cuddles.

But the leafless, ghostly pale, tentacle-like dodder really ramps up the squirm factor. Research has shown it is able to recognize which plants are around it by sense of smell. Every plant gives off a unique blend of compounds such as terpenes, alcohols and esters, making it easy to tell cilantro from tomatoes by just a sniff. Not only can dodder distinguish one plant from another, it can sense which is more nutritious, 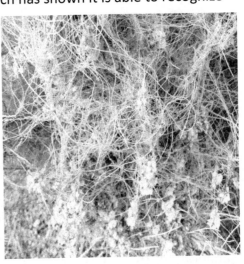 and will move toward that one with great precision, and attack it.

In the words of Consuelo De Moraes, an assistant professor of entomology at Penn State who studies parasitic plants, dodder "exhibits an almost animal-like behavior." It's enough to make you afraid to stand still in the garden for very long.

Because it lacks chlorophyll, dodder needs to vampirize other plants in order to live and reproduce. With the exception of grasses, it can parasitize nearly any plant, but it is especially fond of tomatoes, potatoes, azaleas, legume forage crops, dahlias, petunias, and ivy. Once it reaches its intended victim, dodder inserts root-like filaments called haustoria into the phloem vessels of its prey and begins sucking out nutrient-rich sap. Obviously this is not the best thing for its victims.

In fact it can be devastating. Julie Kikkert, a specialist with the Cornell Vegetable Program, states that a dodder infestation can reduce commercial carrot yields by between 30 and 100 percent. She also notes that dodder produces a tremendous number of seeds very quickly, and that its seeds can remain viable in the soil for as long as 60 years. Obviously, long crop rotation is not a practical way to manage this pestilence.

It turns out that dodder is a real challenge to control. If you find it in your garden or landscape, hand-pull it as best you can. Then prune out and destroy all plants that it has parasitized. Vegetables may have to be thrown out, but for woody plants, prune back the stem an inch or so from the point where dodder has penetrated it.

Unfortunately, there are few herbicide options. Since a nonselective herbicide kills all types of plants, there are not many situations where that can be used. Ideally, a pre-emergent herbicide (one that inhibits germination) could be helpful, but dodder must be listed on the product label. There is some evidence that corn gluten meal, which is considered nontoxic, might inhibit germination. It is available at some garden centers, and online.

The other meaning of dodder, of course, is to amble weakly; totter feebly. If I reach an age where I hear someone refer to me as a doddering old man, maybe I'll be able to frighten them with a few facts about the devil's shoelaces, the creepy orange-tentacled, plant-hunting vegetable vampire. If I can remember the details by then.

Working the Kinks out of Knotweed

Often termed "bamboo" because of its hollow jointed stems and impressive growth rate, Japanese knotweed (*Fallopia japonica*) is well-established in northern NY. As the name suggests, it's from "away." Native to Japan and Korea, it was imported to the US in the late 1800s as an ornamental.

In its home range it grows in some of the least hospitable sites, including—reportedly—in pure volcanic ash. Compared to that, just about anywhere in our region is a paradise. In back yards and vacant lots, along utility and rail rights-of-way and stream banks, this exotic plant thrives, forming dense thickets. Children love to play in these "forests,"

but most adults aren't keen on having to beat back the invader from their gardens and lawns. But because knotweed can provide instant privacy, some welcome it.

As invasive plants go, it could be worse. Knotweed doesn't blister your skin like giant hogweed and wild parsnip do, or snuff out forest regeneration in your woodlot the way swallow-wort does. It's not poisonous to animals; it is in fact grazed by deer, rabbits and even livestock. Maybe the "best" part is that it produces no viable seed.

And it has some genuine good points. It is a source of resveratrol,

149

a compound which shows promise in the treatment of cancer and heart disease. Its flowers, while unable to beget offspring, still produce loads of nectar and pollen, and are an important late-season nectary (I've been waiting a long time to use that word) for honeybees and wild pollinators. It's also a wild edible, featured in Euell Gibbons' seminal book on the topic, "Stalking the Wild Asparagus." The young shoots taste much like rhubarb, and can even be made into pie.

Of course, knotweed has many strikes against it or folks wouldn't get so agitated when you mention its name. It spreads and is very hard to eradicate. Its tough perennial roots (rhizomes) can snake underground far from the nearest plant and pop up a new shoot 60-70 feet away. Knotweed can be moved accidentally with soil or fill, as a teeny bit of rhizome is all it takes for trouble to start. Its tenacious roots also make it hard to kill. You can smother knotweed for several years only to have it reappear like Houdini when you yank the covering back.

When I moved into my home the whole back side was engulfed by knotweed, as was most of the yard. For six years I mowed weekly, and by year seven it appeared I had triumphed. Then after a summer free of the weed, a number of knotweed shoots, wan and tentative though they were, arose the following spring. (They're gone now.)

Arduous as that may seem, I actually consider knotweed one of the easier invasive plants to manage on dry ground. But in riparian habitats, i.e. along waterways, it is a true monster. Its superpower? A tiny fragment of stem, root or leaf, so long as it stays moist, quickly becomes an impenetrable jungle.

Fluctuating water levels wash plant fragments downstream, creating innumerable knotweed colonies. In some stretches of the Oswego and Salmon Rivers, the banks are literally walls of Japanese knotweed. It restricts—sometimes eliminates—water access, and out-competes existing vegetation. Because its tops die back each fall it does not mitigate erosion the way native shoreline plants like willow and shrub dogwood do, and water quality and habitat suffer.

Knotweed infestations in riparian habitats may need to be chemically treated by a professional, but this is not the case with backyard knotweed. Chemical-free methods include repeated hand-pulling (where practical), multi-year mowing, and smothering. And possibly, nonstop pie making.

Let Them Eat Wood

What does a grapple-boom excavator, a termite, and a person enjoying a plate of ginger-shiitake chicken stir fry have in common? They all eat wood. Sort of. At least if you go along with my rather broad definition of eating.

A grapple boom has a powerful hydraulic pincer that can quickly reduce a wood-frame structures to splinters, usually with permission from their respective owners, by chewing through them from the top down. The houses, that is, not the owners.

Unlike carpenter ants, which merely tunnel through wet and decaying wood to make nests, termites actually ingest perfectly sound wood. Technically it is the microbial community in their gut which digest the cellulose and release byproducts that termites depend on. No termite could survive on a diet of wood without its internal "farm" of microorganisms.

And from studio apartments to five-star restaurants, people the world over consume all manner of delectable dishes featuring second-hand wood. Although that is not generally how it is worded on the menu. Mushrooms such as inky cap, oyster and shiitake

have a voracious appetite for wood, a substance that very few organisms eat because it is so hard to digest. Anyone who has tried a two-by-four can attest to that.

Wood is made primarily of cellulose along with varying amounts of lignin. This latter compound is to cellulose what steel reinforcing rod is to concrete. There is far less of it but it imparts a great deal of strength and resilience. Even professional wood-eating bacteria in the gut of a termite can't digest lignin—only a select group of fungi are endowed with that ability.

There are three basic groups of wood-decaying fungi: soft-rot, brown-rot and white-rot. In scientific terms these coteries are not closely related even though they have the same last name. (Apparently for fungi, "rot" is like our "Smith" in that respect.)

Soft-rot fungi are very common, causing garden-variety decay in tomato stakes and fence posts. Wooden ones, at least. Brown rot is less common, though at some time or other you've probably seen its handiwork. This fungus creates a blocky pattern, turning wood into miniature, spongy brown bricks. While brown rot needs moisture to do its dirty work, it is sometimes called dry rot because it readily dries out and is often seen in that condition. Both soft-rot and brown-rot fungi consume only cellulose, eating around the lignin.

White-rot fungi, on the other hand, belong to the clean plate club, digesting both lignin and cellulose. This category of fungi can cause serious decay in hardwood trees, although a few species attack conifers. Foresters hate it, but foodies love it. It is the group that gives us *Armillaria mellea*, a virulent and devastating pathogen, but one which produces tasty honey mushrooms.

Shiitake and oyster mushrooms are white-rot fungi, although they are saprophytes, akin to scavengers like turkey vultures, rather than predator-like pathogens. So we don't have to feel guilty about eating them. Regionally, shiitake farming has, um, mushroomed over the past decade. It is a source of supplemental income for farmers and a source of fun and good food for anyone who wants to try it.

Somewhat fickle, shiitake prefer oak, beech, maple and ironwood, more or less in that order. To cultivate this mushroom, you would cut logs, or bolts, of one of these hardwoods. Bolts are typically about four feet long and range from three to eight inches in diameter. A log will bear mushrooms for roughly one year per diameter inch. A series of holes are drilled in the logs, and these are filled with mushroom "seeds" called spawn. Oyster mushrooms are more laid back, and will grow on less-valuable material such as poplar, or even on a damp roll of toilet paper. They also can be "seeded" between stacked blocks of wood, making it easier to get them started.

Nearly all historians agree Marie Antoinette probably never said "Let them eat cake," a saying already in popular culture before the French Revolution. The phrase was ascribed to her by opponents in order to bolster her reputation as callous and arrogant. She would have seemed far more benevolent if she had said "Let them eat wood."

Chapter Five

Weather

It seems like most weather-related observations have to do with winter, probably because I notice it more.

Snow Jobs

Where agriculture is concerned, dairy is king (or is dairy queen?) in northern NY State. But when we have an unusually snowy winter, it makes me wonder if we shouldn't start producing other crops, ones particularly suited to our region. How about we raise snow peas. Or iceberg lettuce, perhaps. OK, so I'm indulging one of life's most futile activities, griping about the weather. But for farmers, foresters and gardeners, there is an up-side to loads of snow.

Snow has been called "the poor person's fertilizer" because it's a source of trace elements and more importantly, of plant-available forms of nitrogen, a nutrient often in short supply. When snow releases a whole winter's worth of nutrients in a short time, the nitrogen value can add up.

Since air is 78% nitrogen, you'd think plants would have all they need. But atmospheric nitrogen gas, N_2, is a very stable, inert molecule that plants are unable to use. And, it is broken. Sort of. Certain soil bacteria, primarily those which colonize legume roots, can "fix" gaseous nitrogen, converting it to water-soluble forms that plants can slurp up. Lightning also turns nitrogen gas into plant "food." But this only accounts for a small percentage of the nitrogen found in snow.

Turns out snow is a better fertilizer today than it was years ago. There is an outfit called the National Atmospheric Deposition Program (NADP), which basically measures stuff that falls out of the sky that is not some form of water. According to the NADP, the vast majority of snow-borne nitrogen comes from pollution.

Coal-burning power plants and motor vehicles spew out various nitrous oxides, not great for us to breathe, but when washed into the soil, act as nitrate fertilizers. Ammonia, another form of plant-available nitrogen, escapes from manure and commercial urea-based fertilizers.

So how much fertilizer is in the snowdrifts these days? Because the Northeast is the "beneficiary" of more pollution than most of the West and Midwest, we get more nitrogen in our snow than the national average, somewhere around 12 pounds per acre annually. Depending on the crop, a farmer may apply on the order of 150 lbs. of nitrogen per acre, so 12 lbs. is small potatoes. Literally. But it's not chopped liver, either (which is high in nitrogen but not an ideal soil amendment).

Snow-based nitrogen can be a significant boon to ecosystems on marginal soils. In a year with abundant snowfall, sugar bushes, timber lands and pastures undoubtedly benefit from "poor person's fertilizer." Snow brings a fair bit of sulfur, which is an essential plant nutrient. Sulfur also can make soil more acidic, which isn't always a good thing, so let's call it a mixed blessing.

Obviously, snow provides soil moisture in early spring. What is different about snowmelt as compared to rain is that snow melts gradually enough that nearly all its moisture gets into the soil. This gentle percolation is in contrast to summer rain, a percentage of which—sometimes a large portion—runs off and doesn't benefit the soil.

When topsoil is saturated, or as agronomists put it, at field capacity, excess water seeps down through the soil profile. Eventually it becomes groundwater, raising the water table and recharging our aquifers. Nearly all water wells in the region tap into unconfined aquifers. This just means that the water that goes into the ground in a given location is the water that comes out of the well there. These aquifers depend on snowmelt as well as prolonged heavy rains of spring and fall for recharge.

Those who work in field and forest should take heart at the mounting snowbanks, not despair of them. Now if you'll excuse me, I'm headed to the garden with the rototiller to plow up some snow. I'm pretty sure I have a packet of Mixed Frozen Vegetables seeds around here somewhere...

Light Shows

"Solar Max." If there isn't one already, there ought to be a band by that name. Or maybe a renewable-energy superhero. Solar max, or maximum, refers to the period of high sunspot activity in the sun's approximately 11-year solar cycle, and it is usually a time when we see the northern lights, or aurora borealis, more often.

157

Energy that constantly emanates from the sun in the form electrons, x-rays, gamma rays, UV light, visible light and other forms of radiation is referred to as solar wind. While there's always a breeze, sometimes the wind kicks up, and every so often a storm develops. No one knows what causes solar storms, but astronomers can "spot" when one is brewing.

All stars eventually develop spots. Some pout and slink off for cosmetic surgery. Other stars, our sun for example, produce areas of intense magnetic activity—sunspots—on a regular basis. It's not certain if they actually cause other powerful phenomena,

but sunspots almost always appear just prior to solar flares and coronal mass ejections (CMEs). Flares and CMEs are "wind gusts" of solar radiation which emerge from areas near sunspots. The radiation they thrust into space is also known as plasma.

If astronomers observe unusually large sunspots, they keep an eye out for subsequent activity. When a strong CME erupts, it sends high-energy plasma in our direction at speeds of up to 1,800 miles per second. In roughly 24 hours this blast reaches Earth and reacts with its outer atmosphere to produce a geomagnetic storm.

When our favorite sun hurls lethal radiation towards us, we can thank our lucky stars we have a molten core with a high percentage of iron. Or at least that our planet does. This core induces a magnetic field around Earth, thus deflecting radiation and saving us from becoming the toast of our town. As the stream of radiation bends around Earth like water around a rock, some charged particles are "herded" toward the north and south poles, resulting in the aurora borealis and aurora australis, respectively.

Geomagnetic storms don't just put on psychedelic light shows. They're capable of real mischief, and can harm or even disable satellites. In most cases satellites can be moved out of harm's way, or at least turned to shield their solar panels. Storms can also damage electric devices and infrastructure. In March 1989, a geomagnetic storm shut down Hydro-Quebec's state-of-the-art power grid within seconds of hitting Earth, creating a record outage that left six million customers without power. Radio and cell phone transmission was also interrupted, and the aurora borealis was seen as far south as Texas.

The most famous solar event occurred in September 1859 following two massive, consecutive solar flares. Telegraph systems failed. The aurora borealis was seen in the tropics, and in the northeast was bright enough to read by. In 2013, Lloyd's of London calculated that such an event today would cause 2.6 trillion dollars in damage. A Metatech study concluded the world's electric grid could be out for several months, with losses even higher than that. I wonder if that includes deleted Bitcoin currency.

For all the time and effort that goes into studying solar phenomena, much is yet unknown, such as why auroras are more active around the time of the equinoxes. If you don't mind spoiler alerts you can go to noaa.gov and check the space weather forecast, which will indicate if an aurora is expected on a particular night, and presumably if you'll need your space heater.

Frosted by the Weather

When the thermometer starts dipping into negative values at night, and only rises into the single digits during the day, the morning may come when our car, smart phone, water pipes, fingers and/or other essentials have frozen and refuse to work.

It's easy to get so "frosted" by winter's hardships that we miss its artistry. Given the right conditions, though, winter frost can transform the world overnight with a breathtaking majesty that would melt any heart.

Naturally, we tend to associate frost with the "bookends" of winter when the seasons are changing. The frosted lawn in April or October is neither unusual nor very interesting, at least not without a hand lens to see better detail. But mid-winter frost, while not as common, can be truly extravagant.

The kind of frost that turns any landscape into a winter magic-land is called hoarfrost, "hoar" being Old English for grizzled. Hoarfrost occurs in supersaturated conditions when the relative humidity is more than 100%. This may sound like an impossibility, but in fact it's common, at least for short periods of time.

Warm air can hold much more water vapor than cold air, so as the temperature falls in a humid air mass, relative humidity increases, eventually exceeding 100%. Supersaturated water vapor is an unstable condition, and nature is keen to restore balance by shedding moisture. On a cool summer evening that would be in the form of dew, and on a frigid winter night it's hoar frost.

Those fortunate enough to live near a fast-flowing stream or river that stays open in the winter are treated to hoarfrost fairly often, as the open water provides necessary water vapor. Bodies of open water create moist air on a local level, but weather fronts can spread moisture, and thus hoarfrost, over a wide area.

In great literature and children's stories alike, the theme of redemptive transformation is both compelling and appealing. Cinderella's Fairy Godmother changed a pumpkin into a stagecoach, and mice into fine horses. She has nothing on hoarfrost, however, which I think must have learned its craft from the angels themselves.

As water vapor condenses onto cold surfaces, it applies layer upon crystalline layer of fragile, feathery, exquisite ice forms. Even the most ordinary and neglected objects—the weed patch, the tangle of rusty barbed wire—are redeemed by hoarfrost's magic wand. But given a medium that's more complex, more inherently eye-pleasing such as a tree branch, the effect is all the more inspiring. When that effect is multiplied along fencerows and riverbanks, illuminated by morning sun, one has the urge to kneel on the spot and put a hand to one's heart.

You can make ersatz hoarfrost by gathering together cold temperatures, water vapor and a substrate on which to collect ice crystals. The first is easy—we have plenty of cold these days. Water vapor, which can be an uncovered stockpot of water fresh off the wood stove, needs to be concentrated in an unheated garage, enclosed porch or outbuilding. By definition, every object is a substrate, but more intricate objects result in more elaborate crystal formations.

This might have to wait if you first need that pot of boiling water to thaw out those water pipes in the crawl space under your kitchen. While doing so, please keep in mind that "hoarfrost" is not an expletive.

Winter Swings

"Make me one with everything." If you had to guess, you'd probably say that was either a request to a short-order cook, or a supplication to the Divine. More and more often, Mother Nature makes us a winter with everything. It's as if she glances at her weather playlist and hits the keys for unseasonable warmth, extreme cold, high winds, rain, sleet, ice, and snow, selects the "shuffle" function, and goes on vacation.

After each meteorological mood swing I hear people comment how confused the weather makes them feel. You might plant daffodil bulbs on Christmas, shovel heavy snow the next week, then have to buy crampons a few days later because it rains and then suddenly freezes. If you think it's hard for us humans who can retreat into our posh shelters, imagine how the animals feel.

Potsdam, NY's Ken Kogut, a retired Wildlife Biologist from the New York State Department of Environmental Conservation, explains that "The depth and character of snow has a profound impact on wildlife." We can probably understand how deep snow might keep deer from finding food, in addition to hampering their movement. As the snowpack gets sixteen or more inches deep, their bellies drag, and it's hard for them to raise their legs high enough to take a step.

In these conditions, deer will "yard up," finding shelter in a conifer stand. These places have much less snow on the ground because the dense canopy intercepts a lot of the snowfall. The problem is that there is very little to eat, and they may starve to death.

Kogut points out that while it might not be as obvious, in harsh winters a lot of turkeys also starve to death. Typically they forage by walking, scratching at the duff to unearth food, but they are unable to do this in deep snow. They will seek berries that may remain on shrubs and trees like highbush cranberry and hawthorn, but this food is limited.

Some creatures depend snow for survival. Small rodents, meadow voles in particular, fare well in in the world under the snow, which science nerds call the subnivean environment. They're safe from birds of prey, their most significant predators, and can find plenty of weed seeds and other vegetation on which to feed. Unfortunately, this sometimes includes the bark of small tree trunks, much to the disappointment of orchardists and homeowners. However, in parts of the Adirondacks, the American (pine) marten hunts rodents under the snow.

Showshoe hares, with their fur-festooned oversize feet, have an edge in deep snow over predators such as dainty-footed foxes. But with alternate-week thaw cycles, that advantage melts away. And how about species who change into white for the winter? Camouflage doesn't work so well for ermines and hares when Ma Nature keeps swapping out the background color.

The effects of winter weather are not limited to land animals. According to J. Bernard "Bud" Ziolkowski of Saranac Lake, a former Paul Smith's College instructor with a background in fisheries biology, a few fish normally die every year as a result of winter conditions. In winters with a long period of ice cover, though, oxygen in the water can become so depleted that large numbers of fish can suffocate.

Oxygen enters the water in two ways, through surface contact with air, and from aquatic plant photosynthesis. Thick ice cuts off sunlight to plants, and of course there is no contact between water and air. Fish aren't the only ones using oxygen under the ice—decaying vegetation in the bottom sediments (the benthos, to science eggheads) use up far more than the fish do.

At least Mother Nature hasn't given us a winter tornado. But I'm knocking on wood here.

An Ill Wind

The saying "It's an ill wind that blows no good" is meant to remind us that in the midst of adversity we often find hidden gifts. However, a strong wind is sometimes what makes us ill. In certain weather conditions, air becomes laden with positively charged ions, which is not  a plus, as they adversely affect our mental and emotional well-being.

Positive ions are all around, but in blustery conditions, especially in low humidity and moderate temperatures, they are abundant. Strong wind can strip away a negatively-charged electron from nitrogen, oxygen and other well-behaved neutral air molecules, changing them into positive ions which can do odd things. For instance, a friend in southern France recently told me of his neighbor who becomes largely disabled by seasonal mistral winds there. Until they blow over, she is too disoriented to drive or go to work. Science has not been able to explain exactly why too many positive ions in the air are a negative for us, but it has confirmed that the effect is real.

Periods of relentless wind can occur anywhere, but annual tempests in some parts of the world have merited names. The Chinook is well-known to residents of southern Alberta, although it has been felt as far north as High Level. Chinooks have caused 50-degree temperature spikes overnight, and once produced a 170 km/hr gust in Lethbridge. Italy suffers through the sirocco. The sharav afflicts Israelis; Western Europeans persevere through the Föhn, and the American Southwest endures the Santa Ana.

References to "evil" or "devil" winds can be found in centuries-old documents, and oral traditions from regions around the globe include tales of persistent winds driving people mad. Until the early 1980s, however, most of the scientific world dismissed regional tales of havoc wrought by gusty weather as folklore.

Although solid research on the human-health effects of wind dates back to the late 1960s in Israel, peer-reviewed scientific papers began appearing in journals starting around 1980. Since then, studies continue to bolster the concept that there are physical and psychological consequences of bad air.

165

A New York Times article published on October 6, 1981 mentions an Israeli study which found that during the sharav, "...30% of the [Israeli] population becomes ill with migraine, nausea, vomiting, irritability, dimness of vision, respiratory symptoms and other [sharav-induced] effects." The same article cites a report from the Journal of Personality and Social Psychology. In it, Dr. Jonathan M. Charry of Rockefeller University stated that experiments found "The apparent effects of positive ions included increased...irritability as well as a slowing of reaction times...Scores showed an increase in tension, inattention and fatigue."

In a 1983 Austrian study, 2,400 of 3,000 subjects with wind-related malaise had above-normal blood sedimentation rates, a marker usually associated with infection. Work done in 2008 at the Center for Integrative Psychiatry in The Netherlands concluded that, even after adjusting for other weather variables, wind direction had a notable effect on mental health; specifically, a southeasterly wind raised anxiety and lowered energy levels. In other words, it blew no good.

It is important to note that not all people are affected by wind. In fact, most research seems to show that only about one-third of the population is impacted. But that one-third should be happy to learn their weather-induced complaints are not in their heads. On their heads, maybe.

In the words of Bill Puzzo, Professor of World Geography at Cal State Fullerton, as quoted in a 1988 Los Angeles Times article: "...an excess of positive ions tends to almost literally overcharge them [people] with electrical energy. Their hair will have a tendency almost to stand on end..." In sum, an ill wind can cause bad hair, irritability, fatigue, migraines—and fan tragic fires.

166

Thundersnow

New York State's "rooftop" counties bordering the provinces of Ontario and Quebec get plenty of snow, but nothing compared to the region along eastern Lake Ontario known as the Snow Belt. One of the perks of living in that lake-effect zone is, in addition to bragging rights about snowfall amounts and winter-hardiness, a phenomenon called thundersnow. (Turns out that being able to snowshoe up to your second-story window doesn't qualify as a perk.)

It sounds like an awesome name for a band or a snowmobile race, but thundersnow is just a snowstorm with some thunder and lightning thrown in. Presumably Santa is familiar with this type of storm, because he calls two of his reindeer  Donner and Blitzen, names derived from the Dutch words for thunder and lightning, respectively. Though not as exceptional as flying reindeer, thundersnow is fairly uncommon worldwide. But during lake-effect snowstorms in the Great Lakes region, such events may occur many times per season. In most, but not all, cases that season is winter.

In the Iroquois, or Haudenosaunee, tradition, the storytelling season comes to an end after the first thunder of the year. I don't know what kind of a wrench wintertime thunder throws into the works, though. For those Haudenosaunee who love storytelling (all, I assume), one good thing is that when lake-effect snow falls at a rate of four inches per hour, it makes a heck of a good acoustic blanket. The sound of thunder during a snowstorm is muffled and only carries a short distance—a mile or less—unlike summer thunder, which may be audible for five to ten miles.

Lake-effect snow occurs when cold air passes over an expanse of relatively warm water. These events can produce freakishly heavy rates, and thus accumulations, of snowfall. Thundersnow sometimes generates round lightweight ice pellets that look much like Styrofoam beads used in packing. They also feel like packing beads, except colder. These pellets are known as graupel, a German word meaning "packing pellets for beer coolers," or something like that, I assume.

Lightning in winter is potentially as dangerous as it is in summer, except that not quite as many people are out swimming, golfing or picnicking. According to the National Lightning Safety Institute, lightning fatalities do occur during thundersnow. The winter of 1996 saw at least two lightning-caused deaths, and four teenagers sledding in Maine were struck in 2002. Because of the sound-dampening effect of snow, there is little warning of a storm approaching. People are not able to hear thunder and take cover until lightning strikes are close by.

Although the lake-effect snow regions of upstate New York see more than their fair share of thundersnow (and snow, deicing salt, snow, road closures, snow, snow, etc.), consider these facts: The World Meteorological Organization reports that Kampala, Uganda has on average 280 thunderstorms per year. And in the winter of 1971, Mt. Rainier, WA was pummeled with 1,224.5 inches of snow. In light of this I'd say snow-belt residents have nothing to complain about. But then they don't tend to complain anyway.

Thunder or no thunder, if you travel to a snow-belt region this winter, remember that all-season tires are only all-season in climates where it never snows. A two-wheel drive car with good snow tires can often outperform a 4x4 with "all-season" tires.

Hurry Up Already with Global Warming

I had such high hopes for global warming, but winters continue to dish up cold spells here and there. I feel disappointed, betrayed, even. I thought the planet was heating up. All my plans for a northern NY citrus and banana orchard, out the window.

Turns out it's easy to mix up climate and weather, two very different things. There's a saying in the Adirondacks, and elsewhere, I'm sure, that if you don't like the weather, wait five minutes. That's weather: what we experience in a given day, week, season or year.

Climate, on the other hand, refers to long-term trends in weather patterns over decades and centuries. When you have a hundred years of weather records in hand (which we do, and then some) you can begin to look for patterns in climate.

Consider average life expectancy in the US. We know it has steadily risen for the past couple centuries, and is now roughly 79 years. Yet we all know people who, sadly, have died at a much younger age. While unfortunate, this doesn't reflect the long-term trend.

Long-term climate trends going back thousands of years can be gleaned from air trapped in ice cores and pollen trapped in lake sediment cores. Of course, you have to take scientists' word on that sort of thing, and rumor has it some of them favor progressive politics.

It's unlikely that thermometers have a secret political agenda, though, and reliable temperature records date back to about 1850. The consensus of these impartial instruments is that the average temperature of our planet has definitely risen over the last century.

The term 'global' can make climate change seem distant. Climate researcher Dr. Curt Stager of Paul Smith's College points out a number of effects close to home. For example, local records document that our region is about two degrees warmer than it was just fifty years ago.

Lake Champlain ice data, which reach back more than 200 years, indicate in the 19th century there were only three years in which the lake didn't freeze over. But in the 20th century the lake failed to freeze in twenty-eight winters, mostly since 1950.

This warming has wrought other changes. We now get three more inches of precipitation per year than in 1970, resulting in water level rises in lakes and ponds whose outflows are not artificially controlled. Lake Champlain has risen a whole foot in the past forty-five years.

Many people are asking where all the heat goes in cold snaps, a fair question. The coldest air in the northern hemisphere is usually found—no surprise—near the North Pole. Dubbed a "polar vortex" in the 1950s, a large Frisbee of frigid air normally hovers over the arctic quite reliably. On occasion this bitter-cold beanie gets whacked by the jet stream and slips down the face of the planet, bringing the arctic to us.

When we are colder than usual, it is important to remember that many places will be hotter than average. It's a big planet, or so

I'm told. World-wide, average temperatures continue to trend up. Unfortunately the math is not always in our favor.

Weather or Not

Weather modeling has become quite a big deal in recent years, with meteorologists falling all over themselves to report what the latest models say. It sounds like a fun job, and I am trying to find

out how to apply for a position. No doubt I could model categories like "large stationary front" or "high pressure system" pretty well. If it involves appearing in a swimsuit, though, forget it.

I love it when a radio announcer chirps "clear and sunny" during a storm because they read the outlook without a look out. Funny how reality can boost the accuracy of weather reports. So when you can't even bank on today's forecast, it's normal to view long-range projections with a skeptical eye. However, seasonal models are very good at foreseeing key trends such as droughts or severe hurricane seasons. You can depend on models if they call for above-average precipitation this winter. But if you want to know if it will snow on a given day, you'll have to listen to the radio. Or flip a coin.

On its website, the US National Oceanic and Atmospheric Administration (NOAA) explains that seasonal modeling

"...provides information about the expected state of regional climate, based on long-term trends, shorter-term persistence in the climate system, and the current and anticipated state of tropical sea surface temperatures (i.e., El Niño). Seasonal forecasts for upcoming months use sophisticated computer models, statistical models, and/or expert judgments." El Niño and La Niña, respectively, are the warm and cool phases of the 2- to 7-year "Southern Oscillation," a tropical ocean current system that has a huge effect on our weather. That's a drawback to living on a planet—heat doesn't stay on its own part of the map.

Meteorology dates back to Aristotle; in fact he's the guy who came up with the name. I suspect that in its early days, the science was hampered by a noticeable lack of meteors. Honestly, you have to wonder what Aristotle was expecting. Things picked up when meteorology began looking at other stuff that fell out of the sky, rain for example. I had always equated the science with forecasting, since the person on TV giving the weather was called a meteorologist. But the discipline includes studying the chemistry and physics of the atmosphere, and tracking changes and trends in its composition and behavior.

Austria opened the first-ever national weather bureau in 1851, followed by the UK in 1854, and the US in 1890. While virtually every country now has its own weather forecasting service, some of the top research facilities are in China, Japan, France, and the UK. Long-range modeling is an international effort, as getting accurate forecasts is important for all nations. NOAA is a free, user-friendly resource, and I encourage people to visit http://www.cpc.ncep.noaa.gov/products/predictions/long_range to see its outlook for the upcoming season.

Some climate centers charge fees to release modeling charts and graphs. Highly accurate systems such as the European Seasonal to Inter-annual Prediction (EUROSIP) may run 20 or more models at once, each using different processes, and with origins in perhaps a dozen countries. EUROSIP reports are for professionals, with language like "The set of dynamical and statistical models predict weak La Niña conditions with an SST anomaly in the Nino3.4 region of -1.1 C..." I'll stick with NOAA.

Model accuracy is checked by "hindcasting," or predicting past weather. This sounds like another job I could handle, provided the past was not older than about a week. In hindcasting, climate inputs from a given time period are entered into each model, and researchers compare the modeled forecasts with known historical conditions. Models are constantly adjusted to further "train" them. In one exercise, ocean surface temperature readings were used to "forecast" El Niño and La Niña events from 1857 to 2003. Not only did the model correctly identify every event, it predicted each one up to two years out.

Results like that make me wonder why the three-day forecast is often not much better than a guess. Maybe I really should get into weather modeling. I hope you're not required to wax.

Chapter Six

Arthropods

This is a scientific term for "Things Having Way Too Many Legs." I may throw a worm in the mix as well.

Be Nice to Spiders...Or Else

Spiders can be dangerous, but mostly in ways you would never imagine.

A couple of years ago a guy in Seattle burned his house down trying to kill spiders with a blowtorch. In 2015 at a Michigan gas station, a man tried to kill one with a lighter and burned up a pump island, narrowly escaping injury. And Mazda had to recall 42,000 of its vehicles in 2014 because spiders could clog a small fuel vent line with silk, potentially cracking the gas tank and causing a fire. It's no wonder we are afraid of spiders.

Fear of spiders is so common and widespread, and may well be encoded in our DNA. Obviously it would have behooved early humans to learn to be wary of spiders, as a few species are poisonous. Mind you, it's a tiny minority, but spiders can be hard to tell apart. If something with way too many legs and eyes scurries up our leg, most of us will swat first and ask questions later. It's a rare person whose first reaction is "Great—hand it over so I can key it out!" when their partner announces there's a big spider in the bed. You know that person is a hardcore nerd. And that they probably have a relationship issue to work out if they don't want to sleep alone that night.

Worldwide, about 35,000 species of spiders have been identified and named, although there are undoubtedly many more kinds out there running around without a fancy Latin label stuck to them. Roughly 3,000 species call North America home, and of them, only about a dozen are poisonous. New York is host to only one species of toxic spider, while Texas has collected eleven, almost the whole set. But then, they do everything in a big way down there.

Sources don't agree exactly, but apparently we have close to thirty different species of spiders in the Empire State, with eleven of those considered "common." You'd think that in higher latitudes we might be exempt from poisonous spiders; after all, most of them live in hot places. But as it happens the lone species of concern in New York, the northern black widow (*Latrodectus variolus*), is just as happy in the Adirondack and northern tier regions as it is in Long Island.

An interesting sidebar about black widows—so called because they are known to eat the male after mating—is that such behavior is not as common as was once thought. This "sexual cannibalism" (an actual scientific term) was first seen in the lab where males couldn't get away. Seems that in the wild they adhere to a "best defense is a running head start" school of thought, and most of them survive.

A red and black color scheme on a car is cool. On a spider it's scary. Lucky for us, to identify the northern black widow we don't have to flip her upside down to look for the characteristic red hourglass shape on her abdomen. The way I figure it, most bites probably result from people trying to find out if that shiny black spider is poisonous or not. Anyway, the northern species has plenty of bright red geometric patches on her backside in addition to the mark on her belly.

Although black widows have the most toxic venom, the brown recluse spider (*Loxosceles reclusa*) is more dangerous. Brown recluse bites, while rare, often require medical intervention because they cause significant tissue death (necrosis) with potential infection and scarring. In about one percent of cases, their bites lead to death if the venom becomes systemic. Most of these situations involve the elderly or small children.

Here in New York we have no resident brown recluse spiders, which are found from coast to coast but are concentrated in the Midwest. Their range extends from the Gulf States as far north as Virginia (apparently they have good border controls there). Every year, though, a few end up here when they stow away in luggage or gear of returning vacationers. Brown recluses are tan and shiny, not hairy. They have a darker violin-shaped mark on their backs, with the neck of the violin pointing backwards toward the abdomen.

There are aggressive spiders—the invasive hobo spider in the Pacific Northwest, for example—but it should be noted that all of our poisonous ones are docile. Black widows prefer to run away, and the brown recluse (and other recluse spiders) are named that for a reason. It's those unfortunate situations when they hide in a bath towel or clothing and become pinned against human skin that lead to bites.

So how come mystery bites are so often blamed on spiders when most species are not even capable of puncturing human skin? First of all, it is unusual that a victim of a "spider bite" actually saw the culprit. If someone wakes up with a red mark it must have been a spider, right?

To be fair, though, we do have a native spider that can and will bite. Yellow sac spiders (*Cheiracanthium spp.*), common across North America, are ghostly pale, yellow to greenish (sometimes pink or tan), medium-size critters that make little silk homes in curled-up leaves, rock crevices, and occasionally in the corner of a room or in a fuel vent line.

They have a mildly toxic venom that may cause a rash, or in some cases limited tissue necrosis. About twenty-five years ago a yellow sac spider bit the side of my neck (it was in my shirt collar), and an open wound slightly larger than a quarter developed. The lesion turned an alarming gray color and took a couple moths to heal. I have to count my blessings, though. There was no fire.

Damsels and Dragons

You might think a nonfiction essay about damsels and dragons is an oxymoron (or maybe that the author is), or that it sounds like a stale gender stereotype. But dragons are real. Damsels, while appropriately slender, elegant, and arrayed in fancy garb, are not the shrinking violets of fairy tales. They are every inch the airborne flesh-eaters that their chunky dragon cousins are.

We have many species of dragons and damsels, and they emerge at various times throughout the season. On any sunny day between late May and September if you are anywhere near a stream, pond or river, you are likely to see large numbers of shiny red, green or blue flying jewels darting about. It's a treat to watch them snap up insects and, more impressively, mate in mid-air.

Dragonflies and damselflies are carnivorous insects in the order Odonata. Dragonflies are in the sub-order Anisoptera, a term meaning not (an) the same (iso) wings (ptera). Their front pair of wings are longer than hind pair, which is one way to tell them from damselflies, which are in the sub-order Zygoptera in case you were wondering. There are an estimated 6,000 Odonata species in the world, nearly 200 of which have been identified in New York State.

Dragonflies, powerful fliers, can be so large they can look like a bird at first glance. When resting they keep their wings outstretched; a line of them basking on a log seem like small planes waiting to take off. I've been told it's good luck if one lands on you. Probably the "luck" is that they repel deer and black flies.

Damselflies are much more slender than dragonflies. In damsel-like fashion, they fold their wings primly along their bodies when at rest. And while many dragons are colorful, damsels outshine them with bright, iridescent "gowns." Damselflies are sometimes called darning needles, and even the official literature lists such damsel names as "variable dancer" and other descriptive titles.

Both kinds of insects are beneficial in that they eat plenty of black flies, deer flies, mosquitoes and other biting insects. Not surprisingly, they breed in the same habitats as their prey. Damsels and dragons lay their eggs right in the water or on vegetation along streams, rivers or ponds.

The nymphs (immature stages) are monster-like with little resemblance to adults. You can get a sense of what their choppers look like if you watch the movie *Alien*. Seriously, when magnified you can see their primary jaws (actually labia, but they act like jaws) open to reveal a second or even third set of hinged jaws (palps, technically). Depending on the species, nymphs get pretty big—the family Tanytarsidae produce juveniles the width of your hand.

Damsels and dragons spend most of their lives—between one and three years—underwater. Even as youngsters they put a dent in the pest population, gobbling soft grub-like larvae of deer flies and horse flies from the mud and munching mosquito larvae near the surface. They shed their skins, or molt, as many as twelve times as they mature.

Nymphs don't pupate, but when full-grown they crawl from the water, anchor their toenails (tarsal claws) into the nearest tree stump or boat dock, and "unzip" their skin along their backs. Outdoing any science-fiction film, a graceful dragon or damsel emerges from its monster-skin.

After drying its new wings in the sun for a while, these killing machines fly off to eat pests, and of course to mate in a precise and complex ritual. This choreography involves the male passing a sperm packet from his primary genitalia at the end of his tail to a secondary set mid-body, from which the female retrieves it and inseminates herself. All while hitched end-to-end in a "wheel" and engaged in aerobatics. In some species the pair flies in tandem during egg-laying as well.

I hope you get to see plenty of dragons and damsels this season!

Hot Sounds

Probably everyone has a sound they connect with high summer. For me, nothing says "hot" like the drone of a cicada, its song a miniature buzz saw that cuts across a hot afternoon, undulating a bit and then dropping off near the end of its arc. Cicadas are stout, ancient-looking bugs with bulgy eyes and clear wings. While the largest species is about three inches long with a seven-inch wingspan, the ones in our neck of the woods range from 1 to 2.5 inches in length with a wingspan of three inches or so.

It's nearly always the males of a species who develop some loud or gaudy trait to attract a female—they wear bright wing patches, croak loudly, hammer their beaks on dead trees, or even get a mullet and a sports car. True to form, it's the male cicadas who buzz in their bid to attract mates. Unlike crickets and katydids who chirp by rubbing one wing against the other, known as stridulation, cicadas are unique musicians.

Only a committee could have made the noisemaking apparatus of male cicadas more complicated. They have two structures,

181

made of chitin, the same stuff as their exoskeleton, called tymbals. These highly complex organs are low on their abdomen, towards the front. Cicadas contract and relax their abs (finally, a legitimate use for a six-pack) to flex these tymbals against one another to produce clicks. But that's only part of it.

Unlike human males, who are prone to being vacuous between the ears and more substantial in the middle, it's the abdomens of male cicadas which are hollow. This void acts as a sound box much in the way the body of a guitar does.

And the Rube Goldberg music machinery goes on: In the cicada thorax are enlarged cavities that serve as resonance chambers (this smacks of the work of a subcommittee, doesn't it?). These chambers allow a cicada to amplify its call. Then it raises and lowers its abdomen against the branch (or whatever) to further modify the sound. Even if you hate cicada calls, you have to respect the lengths it takes to create them.

In terms of reproductive strategy, cicadas fall into two camps, periodical and annual. It was a real letdown to discover that periodical cicadas do not work in libraries or in the publishing industry. That would be just too cool. They are so called because periodically—every 13 or 17 years, depending on the brood— they complete their life cycle as a group and emerge in droves. Why they elect to come out only in prime-numbered years is anyone's guess. I'd say it's the kind of thing a librarian might opt for.

In northern New York we have annual, or dog-day cicadas, which can be green, brown or black. Ancient Greeks named the hottest part of summer "dog days" because they observed Sirius, the Dog Star, rising at dawn during that time. We get dog-day cicadas every year, but not in such numbers that they're deafening.

182

Whether annual or periodical, cicadas follow the same pattern. Immature or nymph cicadas burrow into the ground and feed on tree roots, either hardwoods like maple and oak, or pine (why spruce and cedar are off the menu I have no idea). According to research, this feeding does no real damage to trees. When they're full-size, nymphs emerge from the soil, climb up on a tree trunk and "unzip" their exoskeleton to reveal an adult. You'll find the empty husks in parks, woods and back yards.

The adults use a syringe-like mouthpart to drink tree sap, but reportedly eat little. They live just long enough to sing, mate and die, dodging predators in between such chores. Given their size, cicadas make yummy prey for birds, reptiles and small mammals. A fearsome-looking giant wasp called the cicada-killer is big enough to grab cicadas and cart them home for baby food. Cicada-killers, while startlingly big, are not aggressive, and stings are unheard of.

Adult cicadas may not feed extensively on trees but they do cause some damage. Mated females use their ovipositors to slice open the bark of a hardwood twig so she can deposit her eggs in the gash. This sometimes causes the twig to break, and if there are a lot of cicadas around it can look like something's wrong with the trees.

Take a minute to appreciate a dog-day song on a sizzling day, preferably in the shade with a cold drink. It won't be long before you'll be wishing for it all back again.

Monster Mosquitoes

Regardless of whether a summer is dry, wet, or average, we still get a healthy crop of mosquitoes. Really all it takes is one or two of the little whiners in your tent to spoil a night's sleep. I'm convinced their ear-buzzing is meant to raise human blood pressure so they can fill up faster. Makes you wish you could somehow ruin their sleep in return.

Well, if they actually slept, there is something that would probably keep them up at night: The Mosquito Monster! Or rather, the monster mosquito, *Psorophora ciliata* (sore AH fur uh silly AHT uh). In addition to terrorizing campers and picnickers, this hulking menace, which is two to three times the size of most mosquitoes, regularly dines on its lesser kin.

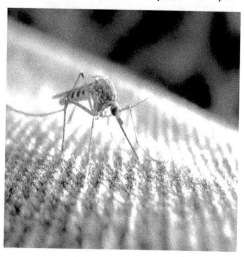

The cannibalism only goes on in the larval stage, but still, when *Psorophora ciliata* touches down, I like to imagine that even full-grown mosquitoes back away slowly, saying hey, this arm's all yours, buddy. I was just leaving anyway and please don't eat me, heh, heh.

It would be comparable to having an eighteen-foot tall biker cut in line at the deli. We would all back down from her. Let's not forget that all those winged vampires are females—the males are strict vegans who eat flower nectar.

Not only is the monster big—well over an inch long, and possessing a 3/8" wingspan—this native 'skeeter is aggressive and delivers an unusually painful bite. Through the years the monster mosquito has engendered more than a few nicknames, most of which are not fit to print. Dubbed the "gallinipper," or "shaggy-legged gallinipper" because of its fuzzy or appearance, *Psorophora ciliata* was described in 1897 by naturalist David Flanery in the journal *Nature* as "...the shyest, slyest, meanest and most venomous of them all."

Depending on environmental conditions and the species, mosquitoes live for as little as a week or as much as a few months, but during that time a single fertile female can potentially spawn thousands of progeny. It is very important to limit the amount of standing water on one's property to help control the mosquito population. Mosquitoes can breed in just a few ounces of the filthiest water. Change pets' water often, and clean their dish between fill-ups, as mosquito eggs can stick to the inside of the container and hatch in the next change of water. The same goes for birdbaths or kiddie pools.

One "nice" thing that you could say about *Psorophora ciliata* is that it isn't known to transmit disease. There are seventy species of mosquitoes in New York State, and only a few of them can carry diseases such as West Nile virus, eastern equine encephalitis, or Zika virus.

Another plus, of sorts, is that the shaggy-legged gallinipper has never become very numerous. In fact, raising *Psorophora ciliata* was once proposed as a method of keeping the populations of disease-carrying mosquitoes in check, but no one could figure out how to produce enough gallinippers to create an effective control.

Whatever the reason they don't breed like flies, we should all be grateful we're not overrun by monster mosquitoes.

Assassins and Hunters Under the Bed

If you announce to your friends that you've seen dust-bunnies under your bed come to life, and that you think masked hunters in the house have been stalking you at night, they'd probably all take a step backward. Until you explained that masked hunters are a type of assassin bug belonging to the order Hemiptera.

Native to Europe and Africa, masked hunters are now widespread throughout North America. These fierce predators of insects and other arthropods get their name from a curious habit of covering, or masking, themselves with dirt and dust as a means of camouflage. Mature adults are shiny black beetle-like insects measuring about three-quarters of an inch long. During their long "childhood," though, masked hunters look neither dark nor shiny.

During their several immature (nymph) life stages their bodies exude a sticky substance, which young masked hunters use to glue fibers from their surroundings onto themselves. (Turns out that it's not just kindergarteners that like to play with paste.) In addition, masked hunters have barbed hairs on their legs, which aid in trapping dust. They do a good camo job, and can look for all the world like animated lint-blobs.

186

Masked hunters are seldom found indoors, and then usually only in small numbers. There are rare exceptions during sporadic "boom" years when their population spikes, and in such a year more of them may be seen indoors. The good news is that even though they're dusty, they'll "clean house" for you. Like most assassin bugs, masked hunters eat pests such as millipedes and bed bugs.

"The good news" is an ominous phrase, indicating bad news will follow. And there are a couple of down sides to having these critters afoot in your home. The first is that masked hunters possess a formidable weapon, a piercing mouthpart called a rostrum. They use this sharp hypodermic needle-mouth to impale their prey and inject a toxin to both paralyze it and liquefy its insides. Even prey larger than they are taken down.

Although they're not aggressive, masked hunters do sometimes bite people when handled, either deliberately or inadvertently. They're most active at night, and although this is rare, they've been known to bite people who groggily brushed away a bug that landed on them as they slept. The bite causes painful swelling that can last up to a week. Such an attack may not be discovered until morning, and since the culprit has fled, the injury may be dubbed a spider bite.

The other down side, if you can call it that, is corollary to the fact masked hunters really like to eat bed bugs. If you have lots of "dust bugs" underfoot, you may also have their favorite—and your least favorite—bedfellow as well. If you find a number of masked hunters indoors, check for the presence of bed bugs. But if you see just one or two, chalk it up as a curiosity that seldom causes problems.

One caveat: should you wish to discuss an assassin called the masked hunter, you probably shouldn't do so when going through airport screening. Unless they're up to snuff on their entomology, security officials might not believe you're talking about a fuzz-festooned Hemiptera that eats bed bugs.

Don't Buy Bad Bugs

Back in "the day" one would see more flea markets, but you don't hear that term so much anymore. No doubt some focus group discovered "flea market" induced a lot of spontaneous itching but little spending. I guess it was possible, if unlikely, to bring home an actual flea with a piece of used furniture. While "rummage sale" is more marketable, there are now concerns about an even worse pest that can hide out in certain pre-owned treasures. In fact, people might get downright nostalgic about fleas now that bed bugs are back.

Although DDT was discovered in the late 1800s, it was not widely used until the 1930s. After World War II its use really took off, and as a result, bed bugs disappeared. But so did eagles and ospreys. In addition, it was found to increase rates of cancer and birth defects, and it was banned for most uses in the US in 1972. Even post-DDT, bed bugs remained off the radar until the late 1990s. Their resurgence in the past fifteen years has taken the public by surprise.

Bed bugs don't spread disease, but they'll bite plenty and keep you up at night. Plus they're just gross. They're not a sign of poor sanitation, and are as likely to be found in a Spartan, spotless home as a cluttered one. The difference is they're easier to get rid of in a clean home.

Despite their name, bed bugs are not limited to beds. We all know to be suspicious of a used mattress, but they can hide in any space wide enough to slide the edge of a credit card into. Besides the obvious culprits like plush furniture, other items like wood bed frames and cribs, luggage and backpacks can also harbor the pests.

This is not to say you ought to avoid buying these items, but that you should take time to examine them before purchase. Adult bed bugs are very flat in profile, and roughly a quarter-inch long. Nymphs range from 1/16th to 3/16th of an inch. After a feeding, they have been described as "a drop of blood with legs."

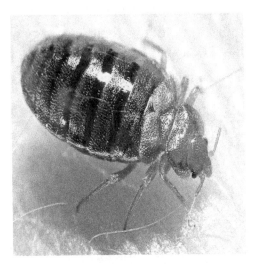

Look closely around piping on cushions and mattresses for brownish-red staining. Bed bug feces look a bit like dots from a fine felt-tip red marker. Check corners and crevices for cast-off skins left behind as they molt. Before carting your rummage-sale find indoors it's probably a good idea to leave it outside to give it a better inspection than you could at the sale. Bed bugs can live for more than a year between feedings, and can even survive below-zero temperatures as long as it gets cold gradually, so don't assume an item that was in a barn over the winter is bug-free.

There are other ways to bring these guys home, of course. They can hide in your book bag, suitcase or purse after visiting hotels, airports, health clubs, laundromats—the list is endless. If you find them in your home, don't panic and throw away your mattress or furniture—that's not necessary and will do nothing to end the infestation. Cornell strongly advises working with a pest management professional, even if you want to avoid chemicals. More often than not, the do-it-yourselfer just prolongs the infestation and winds up hiring a pro in the end anyway.

Sadly, there is more misinformation about bed bugs than on most other home pests. Since I've only scratched (so to speak) the surface of this topic, please go to the U.S. EPA's site at http://www2.epa.gov/bedbugs or another research-based source for detailed accurate information.

Have fun treasure hunting at those rummage sales, and don't let the you-know-whats bite.

Good Bees, Bad Bees

You may have noticed how on sunny warm days in early spring, bees of various stripes come out of the woodwork—sometimes literally. By definition, it's only a "real" bee if it's wearing fur, but not everyone wants to get close enough to see whether or not the thing is covered in minute hairs. If it looks like a bee and buzzes like one, it's OK to call it a bee.

Except for those who are allergic to their stings, most people feel rather warm and fuzzy toward honeybees, or at the very least don't despise them. Their role as pollinators of food crops is widely known, and besides, who doesn't like honey?

Wasps, on the other hand, are generally hated and feared, not necessarily in that order. Social wasps such as yellow jackets, paper wasps and hornets only play nice with their own kind, and are otherwise distinctly antisocial. They can be more dangerous than honeybees because they will vigorously defend their nests. And unlike honeybees, which die after stinging because the stinger and venom sac tear away from their abdomen, wasps can sting repeatedly without paying with their lives.

So what's the deal with wasps—are they just an error in the Creation master plan along with poison ivy and rats, probably the result of some Divine clerical oversight? Actually, they do a lot of good for our planet.

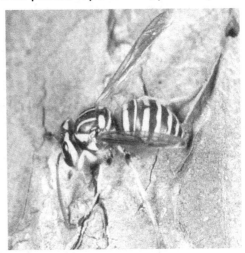

Solitary wasps—which by the way are much more friendly than social wasps—are beneficial because they prey on insect pests like locusts, grasshoppers, and even the dreaded emerald ash borer. Though each female wasp digs her own hole, many nests may be concentrated in one area. You may have crossed a sandy lot in summer and seen holes made by such creatures. (If they were very active at the time, they might have freaked you out.)

After immobilizing a bug with her sting, Ma Wasp carts it home, stuffs it down the nest-hole and lays eggs in it so her babies can hatch and eat their way out of the hapless victim. Beneficial, but not very nice. The largest in our area is the cicada-killer wasp, a fearsome-looking assassin that is completely harmless unless you are a cicada.

On the other end of the spectrum are braconid wasps, so tiny that you wouldn't even recognize them as bees. They don't have the horsepower to bring their victims home, so they lay eggs in a larva or pupa and hope for the best. Braconids are among the most important beneficial insects on Earth.

What may come as a surprise is that wasps are important pollinators. Not to take anything away from honeybees, but those sweethearts are not really that important as pollen couriers. Except in areas of extremely intensive agriculture, their presence or absence has no measurable effect on pollination rates. Bumble bees, mason bees and other native bees, along with wasps, flies and various insects do the job quite nicely so long as they have access to wild, unkempt areas.

In our climate—I should say thus far at least—wasp colonies do not overwinter. Mated queens will seek shelter in leaf litter or rotten stumps, sometimes grouping together in eaves, attics or other hibernacula. So every wasp you see in early spring is a queen seeking to found her own city-state, which may be disconcerting news to some. Take heart; they don't all want to settle on your front porch.

Social wasps are expert paper-makers, chewing up wood and creating beautiful, if terrifying, nests. Paper wasps make open-faced "umbrella" homes, while hornets and yellow jackets make enclosed, globe-shaped nests. Hornets always nest aloft, while yellow jackets usually make underground homes.

Carpenter bees can chew wood like pros, but they skip the paper-making step and just nest in tunnels in decaying trees or perfectly sound soffit and fascia boards on your home or barn. They cause anxiety when the males dive-bomb passers-by, who generally don't know that guys can't sting.

Nests on or near homes may have to be destroyed. But because wasps are so helpful, please consider leaving nests that are not direct risks. You can always try playing them recordings of anger-management programs.

Get Ticked Off

Summer should be a carefree season full of picnics and

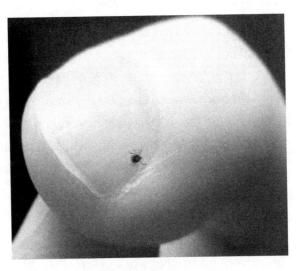

swimming, a time for hikes and barbeques, not a time to fret about tick-borne illnesses. We want limes, not Lyme. Yet we can't afford to stick our head in the sand and ignore the issue. We'd probably end up with grit in our ears, which is uncomfortable. Worse yet, we could contract a tick-borne disease, leaving us too ill to enjoy summer.

As few as twenty years ago it was rare to find even a single tick on your person after a weekend of camping in northern NY State. Now in many places all you have to do is set foot in the brush to get several black-legged ticks, commonly known as deer ticks, which are harder to see than many other ticks.

The deer tick is known to transmit Lyme disease as well as babesiosis, anaplasmosis, Powassan virus and other serious illnesses. In fact it's possible for two or more diseases to be transferred to a host, human or otherwise, by a single tick bite.

Most infections come from an immature or nymph stage deer tick, which can be tinier than a poppy seed and nearly impossible to detect, at least for those of us over fifty, without magnification. The adult tick is not exactly huge, being smaller than a sesame seed. To avoid being bitten by ticks, people who work or play outdoors need to start taking precautions that weren't necessary in the past.

This isn't to say we need to panic, though feel free to do so if you like, of course. According to a study conducted in 2014 in northern NY State, about 50 % of deer ticks are infected with *Borrelia burgdorferi*, the primary spirochete bacterium that causes Lyme (as of 2016, we now recognize two other spirochetes in the same genus which also cause Lyme variants). In most cases, ticks must feed for 24 hours in order to transmit Lyme. And even in the case of transmission, prompt treatment cures Lyme in the majority of infected people.

However, it's not always as simple as taking pills and feeling improvement. Unlike a tissue infection where antibiotics usually provide relief within days, Lyme symptoms can persist for weeks, months, or in some cases years after the standard 4-week treatment has ended. This is called "Post-Lyme Syndrome," and is not well understood. Lyme is not a disease to take lightly.

Avoiding ticks is the first order of business. Ticks "quest" at the tips of tall grass or brush, waiting to cling to the next warm body that brushes against them. The Centers for Disease Control and Prevention (CDC) recommend using products with 20-30% DEET on exposed skin. Clothing, footwear and gear such as tents should be treated with products containing permethrin. Hikers should stick to marked trails.

Homeowners can clear brush, weeds and tall grasses from the edges of their yards. Ticks like to hide under leaf litter, which is why area sprays are not generally effective, so maintaining a yard perimeter that is raked clean can help discourage ticks.

Pets should be treated regularly with an anti-tick product so they don't bring deer ticks into the home. Talk to your vet about getting your pets vaccinated against Lyme.

Despite their name, deer ticks feed on—and infect—many wild critters, especially rodents like our native and ubiquitous white-footed mouse. Because of ticks' prevalence, people who spend a lot of time outside will eventually have contact with deer ticks. This is where tick hygiene comes in.

Shower and wash thoroughly every evening and then check for ticks. Regrettably they like hard-to-see places such as the armpits, groin, scalp and the backs of the knees, so look closely in these areas. If you find a tick has latched onto you, the CDC recommends you grasp it as close to its head as possible with tweezers and pull straight up until it releases. You may have to pull hard if it's been feeding a while. Don't twist it or use heat, petroleum jelly or other home remedies to get it to release, because this increases the chance of disease transmission.

Lyme has no "typical" early symptoms, which vary tremendously from one person to the next. Initial signs may include severe headache, chills, sweats, joint pain, extreme fatigue and malaise. The first inkling you have Lyme may also be cardiac arrhythmia, memory loss, confusion and difficulty concentrating.

Researchers now agree that only about 20% of Lyme cases result in the red, expanding "bull's-eye" rash called erythema migrans that was once considered the hallmark of the illness. Early symptoms may pass, but without treatment, the Lyme organism will cause grave health issues such as arthritis, cardiac damage and debilitating brain injury in the future.

If you've been bitten by a tick and develop any of these symptoms, see your doctor right away. She or he should prescribe antibiotics based on symptoms, as there are currently no reliable tests. For more information, see www.ilads.org.

Do your best to keep yourself and your loved ones ticked off in all seasons.

Move Over, Medusa

As a kid I was fascinated by caterpillars, but had trouble pronouncing the word. To me, the sweet little woolly-bear traversing my hand was a "calipitter." Obviously, a calipitter is an instrument used to very accurately measure the diameter of a caterpillar. Or it will be when someone invents the thing.

Caterpillars continue to interest me, although I no longer find them universally cute. Imagine the loss of innocence after the discovery that some of these fuzzy, fascinating, gentle creatures that tickled their way along my arm were venomous. Certain species have modified hairs that inject toxins under one's skin. This revelation was akin to learning that Bambi was really a brutal carnivore.

It seems a further injustice that many of the so-called "stinging-hair caterpillars" are among the cutest and most colorful out there. But at least they are not aggressive the way yellow jackets can be. They are strictly defensive, the defense being hollow hairs connected to poison glands that secrete toxins. The chemical cocktail varies by species, often involving serotonin, histamine, formic acid and various amino acids, but the result is always painful. While caterpillar hair is far less dangerous than

Medusa's, research suggests that the average person is more likely to meet a caterpillar than a mythical monster.

The hairs (of caterpillars, not Medusa) inject their charge only when the critters are roughly handled. Or fall down your shirt, or wander into your sleeping bag (as happened to one of my nephews one summer), or become pressed against one's skin in some other way. Unluckily the stings cause a painful rash which in some cases may persist for a week or more. A few people have severe reactions which require medical treatment.

One might assume that toxic caterpillars would only be found alongside colorful poison-arrow frogs in the tropics, but we have plenty of native species in our region. One large and diverse group are the tussock moth caterpillars, which look about as terrifying as teddy bears. Two examples are the hickory

197

(*Lophocampa caryae*) and white-marked (*Orgyia leucostigma*) tussock moths, common locally. I've had many encounters with these and other of their kin over the years.

The fluffy hickory tussock moth caterpillar is mostly white, peppered with longer black "whiskers." White-marked tussock moth larvae look like they're fresh out of clown school, having a yellow-and-black striped pattern, a bright red head with a pair of super-long black appendages as a headdress, a row of lateral white hairs on each side, and four bright yellow (sometimes white) toothbrush-bristle tufts behind their heads.

The stubby brown hag moth caterpillar (*Phobetron pithecium*) could easily be mistaken for a dust-bunny or lint ball. Sometimes known as the monkey slug, this oddity has eight furry, arm-like appendages. This makes it resemble a tiny plush toy. If you come across the monkey slug, please resist the impulse to cuddle it.

Similar to the way poison-arrow frogs dress flamboyantly to advertise they are a poor choice as prey, some toxic caterpillars have eye-popping paint jobs. For example, the brilliantly attired stinging rose (*Parasa indetermina*) and saddleback (*Acharia stimulea*) caterpillars look like miniature party piñatas.

Fortunately, many poisonous caterpillars fit the part of villain. The Io (*Automeris io*), a huge moth bearing a striking eye-spot shape on each wing, starts out as a neon-green (red until its first molt) caterpillar teeming with scary-looking barbs. And lucky that the creepy-looking South American giant silkworm moth caterpillar (*Lonomia oblique*), which has caused as many as 500 human deaths, has not yet made its way north.

It is good to note that all caterpillar hairs can induce asthma, because they are very fragile and readily waft on the breeze.

198

Pests such as the eastern and forest tent caterpillars, as well as gypsy moths, can occur in such large numbers that their airborne hairs trigger asthma, especially in children. Even the beloved woolly bears (species in the family *Arctiinae*) can cause attacks.

The best thing to do in case of a sting is to use Scotch or packing tape on the skin to pull out any embedded caterpillar hairs (along with a few of your own). Wash the affected area, and isolate any clothing you suspect may harbor stray hairs. Monitor the affected person for several hours for signs of a serious reaction, but otherwise treat the rash the way you would any sting. Use calamine lotion, antihistamines, or hydrocortisone lotion as directed by your doctor.

Hopefully, having a few bad apples around will not keep you from loving caterpillars. Even the ugliest ones grow up to be moths and butterflies, many of which are beautiful, and all of which are important pollinators. Aside from the ones described above, feel free to investigate all others. And be sure to take along your calipitter in case you want to measure them.

Unfair Accusations

Even though I live in a remote area, I often hear the neighbors arguing as I drift off to sleep. The bickering seems to be fraught with baseless accusations—a real "he said, she said" kind of thing. It doesn't keep me awake or anything, but I wouldn't mind some resolution. I mean, what is it that Katy allegedly did?

Katydids are similar to their cousins the grasshoppers in size and shape, except that they're bright green and have long wispy antennae. Both the male and the female call to find mates, an unusual feature in the insect world where the male is usually the only one who sings. Katydids call by rubbing their forewings together, an act known as stridulation. Their "ears," or tympanic organs, are actually located on their front legs.

Calls vary by species as well as by geographic location. Here in the northern United States, katydids most frequently make an eight-pulse call consisting of three phrases. To many people it sounds like "Ka-ty-did, she did-n't, she-did." Technically it's the male who makes this call, so his argument is really with himself (some readers may not find that surprising). The female responds with a one-note tick, which probably translates to "Humph!"

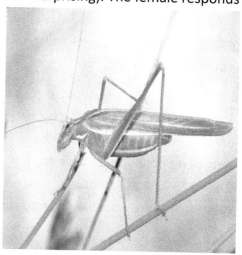

Throughout the world, katydids are both ubiquitous and numerous. In the U.S. we have roughly 100 species, while in the Amazon rainforest there are an estimated 2,000 species. If you've never seen a katydid, you're not alone in that. Because these insects are nocturnal, even entomologists find it challenging to study katydids. In the late 1960s, two entomologists spent months driving along the Appalachian Mountains at night, tape-recording scores of different katydid species' calls. As a result of their arduous and painstaking study, we know more about katydid distribution and interbreeding.

Many species of katydids live in trees. I once stayed in a house built into a hillside, and the screens in the front bedrooms, which were essentially in the treetops, were swarmed by these green insects on summer nights. Although they feed on many types of plants in addition to trees, katydids in our neck of the woods (so to speak) are generally not considered pests. Actually they're an important source of protein for many birds and other small animals.

An old Abenaki friend told me that katydids begin calling about six weeks before the first frost; this way one can tell whether or not it will be a late fall. For a while I would mark on the calendar when the first katydid called, and in my scientifically-unsound sample, the katydids were correct (i.e., Katy did).

Recently I came across a story, attributed to the Cherokee, in which a katydid predicted a hunter's death. It wasn't quite clear to me how that worked, though. Being middle-aged is enough to make me aware of human mortality. I hope to enjoy their song for many summers to come, but in the event I'm faced with a serious health crisis, I won't accuse the katydids of having a hand in it.

Unwelcome Decorations

It's round to oval-shaped, mostly orange, and is a common sight leading up to Halloween. Everyone knows what I mean: *Harmonia axyridis*, obviously. Better known as 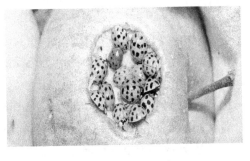 the multicolored Asian lady beetle, this insect is no treat when it masses by the hundreds or thousands on and in homes in the fall.

Lady beetles, or lady bugs, are the darlings of small children everywhere. There are a number of native lady beetle species, which tend to be more red than orange, and they aren't known to be nuisances in homes. Multicolored Asian lady beetles, however, are not as polite.

First brought to the U.S. in 1916 to control pests on pecan trees and other crops, the multicolored Asian lady beetle didn't turn into an ogre until the mid-1990s. Actually there's evidence to suggest that the current population is a new strain accidentally released at the Port of New Orleans in the late 1980s. Whatever their origin, they're back in season each fall along with corn shocks and Jack-o'-lanterns.

Lady beetles don't carry disease, damage structures, suck blood or sting, and their larvae eat harmful garden pests such as aphids. However, they stain surfaces, give off a foul odor when disturbed and will even pinch you on occasion. It's their sheer numbers, though, swarming a sunny exterior wall, massed in a corner of the garage or coating the inside of a picture window, which unnerve and irritate so many people. They are most active on mild days, and may reawaken during any warm spell, even in winter.

The good news is that managing lady beetles will also cut your heating bill. They're looking for someplace warm to spend the winter and if a draft can get in, they can too. Pest-control measures include caulking around windows, vents and places where cable or other utilities come through the wall. Be sure to seal between the foundation and sill. Ensure that door sweeps and thresholds are tight, and check for cracked seals around garage doors. Install screens on attic vents and inspect all window screens.

If the beetles are already indoors, don't swat or crush them or they'll release a smelly and staining yellow defense fluid from their joints (creepy, I know). For a variety of reasons including the lady bugs' habit of seeking inaccessible areas, indoor pesticide use is ineffective, and is strongly discouraged. Instead, use a broom and dustpan or a vacuum cleaner. Try using a knee-high nylon stocking inserted into the hose and secured with a rubber band as a reusable "mini-bag." Just remember to empty it as soon as the vacuum is turned off. You can also find instructions online for making a black light trap.

This fall, I think researchers should try decorating giant pumpkins to look like multicolored Asian lady beetles to see if it will frighten the actual pests away. Hopefully it won't attract a mate of similar size. If you see a 100-pound multicolored Asian lady beetle on Halloween, please don't swat it.

Worms Gone Crazy

If you're tired of hearing about new invasive species, I'm right there with you. Aside from the fact that there is too much bad news around as it is, we're still working those good old-fashioned pests that rival the common cold in terms of eluding conquest. Japanese beetles, European chafers, buckthorn, wild parsnip, Japanese knotweed—enough already.

We don't need a new invasive species every year, but try convincing them of that. I half-expect to get a bulletin one of these days on some tropical soil-shark that stowed away in a shipload of potting mix. Probably it'll feed on moles and woodchucks, but will also burst up out of lawns to swallow small pets, and gardeners might lose a finger while weeding. That would sure put lily-leaf beetles and leek moths in perspective.

So I'd be a lot more hesitant to tell you about a significant new threat to forests, landscapes and gardens if it wasn't for the fact that you can make a real difference in preventing its spread.

While it was once thought this new pest was a single species, *Amynthas agrestis,* we now know it is a number of species from several genera, primarily *Amynthas.* These super-size (eight-inch) earthworms, a.k.a. crazy worms, Asian jumping worms, Alabama or Georgia jumpers, or snake worms, are sold as bait, and sadly are also hawked as a substitute for the harmless red wiggler used in worm compost bins. Crazy worms move rapidly on top of the soil, snake-like, when disturbed. Lively and strong, they can flip out of your hand. Assuming you want to touch them.

Other than the impressive squirm factor—in every sense—these worms are not good for the soil. They're not your grandparents' worms. OK, that didn't come out quite right. Let me rephrase it.

Here in the Northeast where glaciers scrubbed our bedrock bare a few years back we have no native earthworms. There's debate, especially in the forestry world, over just how much of a mixed blessing our European earthworm species are, but I won't get into that. Let's just assume earthworms are good.

Native to Japan and Korea, *Amynthas* and company are very different animals. Their reproduction, for example. Our old-fashioned earthworms are hermaphroditic, outfitted with both male and female organs, but they still need to find a date with another of their kind. Crazy worms, however, are parthenogenic, meaning they're all females that spew out cocoons teeming with baby female worms by the hundreds without needing to mate. Ever. All it takes is one to start an infestation.

They also mature twice as fast as European earthworms, completing two generations per season instead of just one. And their population density gets higher than other worms. And remember they're big.

That adds up to a monstrous worm biomass that can consume virtually all soil organic matter. This includes your lawn and the roots of annuals, perennials and shrubs. In the woods, crazy worms destroy native wildflowers, wiping out trillium, bloodroot, Jack-in-the-pulpit, ladyslipper and other understory plants. Ground-nesting songbirds like the oven bird disappear, too.

When an infestation vacuums organics from soil, it becomes clumpy and granular, prone to compaction and erosion. Forest soils actually subside, exposing tree roots. Wisconsin Department of Natural Resources invasive species specialist Bernie Williams stated bluntly "Their introduction into our state poses a huge threat to the future of our forests."

Crazy snake worms can be distinguished from harmless ones by a band near their middle called a clitellum. In most worms it's thicker than the rest of their body, and of a similar color. In crazy worms it's even with their body, and is milky gray to white in contrast to their dark gray color.

Crazy worms are transplants, and that's how they often spread. Whether in a potted plant from a garden center or a gift from a relative down South, these monsters hitchhike long distances with transplants. They also move from infested areas in shipments of mulch.

There are two ways of telling if your potted plant harbors dangerous fugitives. One is to turn it upside-down and gently remove the root ball. If crazy worms are present, some of the roots, as well as some potting soil, may be missing. The thing is, if only juvenile worms or cocoons are present, damage might not be evident.

Another solution is a mustard solution. Mix a gallon of water with one-third cup of ground yellow mustard seed, and pour this slowly into the soil. It won't hurt the plants, but worms (even "good" ones) will come to the surface and you can check for miscreants.

Because of their acrobatics, crazy worms are valued as fishing bait. This is illegal in most places, but it does happen. To be safe, anglers should securely cover bait containers, and destroy all unused bait by placing it on concrete and crushing it. If you have a household worm bin, only use European red wigglers, *Eisenia fetida*, which won't survive outdoors over the winter.

With a presence in Wisconsin and Minnesota, we know these things are hardy to USDA Zone 4 and possibly colder. Right now there are at least five known infestations within NY's Adirondack Park, and it's likely there are more throughout northern NY State.

If you suspect you may have found crazy worms, please call the proper authorities. If you think it's an invasive soil shark, though, I don't want to know about it.

Don't Flee from These Fleas

If you tromp around in the woods during winter, especially on mild days, you may notice dark specks collecting in depressions in the snow. If you look closely you'll see these little pepper flakes bouncing around. They're called snow fleas, but don't panic—they're not real fleas.

They're not especially fond of snow, either, but other than that, snow fleas are aptly named. On sunny days in late winter they often congregate near the bases of trees or collect in footprints. While snow fleas are the size of actual fleas, they haven't the least interest in you or your pets, but please don't take that personally. Try not to step on them, as they may give us the means to improve both organ transplantation and ice cream.

Snow fleas, a type of "springtail," were classified as insects until recent DNA sequencing pegged them as another type of arthropod called a hexapod. Apparently there's now heated debate as to whether springtails constitute a hexapod class or merely a sub-class. You have to love scientists. First they study an obscure organism to develop life-saving technology, then come to fisticuffs over what to call it.

Whatever their label, snow fleas are beneficial in many ways. As decomposers of organic matter, they help create healthy topsoil.

They and their hexapod cousins are one of the most abundant types of soil "animals," numbering around 100,000 individuals per cubic yard of topsoil.

Besides eating algae, fungi, nematodes, protozoa and a wide range of organic matter, they consume organisms and spores that cause damping-off wilt and other plant diseases. In fact, springtails are being studied for their potential to control disease in greenhouses.

Snow fleas also produce a unique glycine-rich protein that keeps ice from forming inside their cells even at very cold temperatures. This newly discovered molecule is unlike any previously known protein, and is the basis for research on more efficient storage of transplant organs. Organs could be stored for much longer if this protein allows them to be kept at below-freezing temps without damage.

A slightly less important application, but a welcome one to many, is that snow fleas could improve ice cream. Eventually we may see ice cream that never forms ice crystals no matter how long it sits neglected in the freezer.

Springtails lack a respiratory system and must breathe through their skin. As a result, they're quite vulnerable to drying out, and hop around to find moist, sheltered places as well as things to eat.

A true flea uses its tarsi, or toes, to vertically jump as much as seven inches, roughly equivalent to someone leaping 500 feet straight up using only their toes. A snow flea, however, is not nearly so athletic. It can use its two tail-like appendages to bounce a fraction of a flea-jump, comparable to a human leaping a mere dozen feet in the air. I feel so much less inadequate now.

During warmer months, snow fleas and other springtails are more active than in winter, though without a snowy background for contrast they're hard to see. They forage extensively in the humus layer and move throughout the soil profile, even quite deep. Springtails can be found up in the forest canopy as well as on water, where surface tension keeps them from sinking. If you go out with a flashlight some June night you can see springtails bopping about on standing water.

Just hearing the word "flea" can set folks on edge and start them scratching, so it's unfortunate about snow fleas' name. Think of them as springtails, and keep an eye out on bright winter days for these jittery critters that help create topsoil, and could one day help save our life. Or at the very least, our ice cream.

Chapter Seven

Natural Resources

This heading sounds better than "Whatever."

Solving Core Problems

"One if by land; two if by sea." This famous quote is as relevant today as it was on the eve of the American Revolution. Except now it is relevant to the fate of organic waste generated in our kitchens (presumably using Revere Ware). Is land disposal the first choice for an apple core, or should give it a watery farewell down the drain?

It's no surprise that landfills aren't the greenest option. Trucked many miles, buried and compacted by heavy equipment, apple core interments require fossil fuel. And because there's no oxygen within a landfill, organic waste emits methane as it decomposes. It's an excellent fuel, but when released into the air, methane is 25 times more effective than carbon dioxide at trapping greenhouse heat.

However, the EPA requires landfills to capture methane and burn it, often but not always to generate electricity, or tie into a pipeline and sell it to a utility. This positive outcome doesn't get us off the hook. On the balance, it still uses energy to landfill kitchen waste.

Let's try sending organic matter down the drain via a food-disposal unit. This would be ridiculous for anyone on a septic system. Food waste is higher in carbon than sewage, resulting in more residual solids and thus the need for more frequent pump-outs. However, sewage treatment plants are well-suited to handle kitchen scraps. So the village or city dweller might assume the down-drain option is best.

Everything mixed with water and washed down the drain must eventually be taken out of that same water through treatments which take a lot of energy. The process used in most of the Northeast is called "activated sludge." Personally, I favor sludge which is passive and less apt to make sudden moves. Activated-sludge processes require constant aeration and agitation, taking lots of electricity.

Treatment plants emit methane, a portion of which is collected and used for heat and power at large plants. Unfortunately, many small communities in rural regions can't afford to invest in the equipment necessary for methane capture.

Because wastewater treatment can't remove all pollutants, a few oxygen-robbing nutrients from my apple core will end up in surface water bodies; rivers and lakes, helping to trigger algae blooms. In light of of these and other issues like increased water usage, many US jurisdictions as well as several EU countries have banned in-sink garbage disposal units.

A fraction of my garbage-disposal apple core winds up as dried sewage sludge, a treatment byproduct, organic matter with a heavy carbon footprint. Some washes downriver to a lake or ocean, and some becomes methane, helping to cook the planet. Sending stuff down the drain has all the land, sea and air bases covered—in pollution.

Composting, on the other hand, yields rich humus, generates no methane or odors, and you don't need a big back yard—or any yard—to successfully compost. Many home compost systems are suitable for even the tightest living space. Worm composting is an easy, odorless and inexpensive choice, perfect for apartments and other small quarters. It can also be fun and educational for kids. Call your local Extension office for information on how to set up a worm bin or other composting system.

It's hard to choose between two undesirable options, but unless your wastewater treatment plant traps and uses methane, it may be marginally better to toss kitchen waste in the trash to keep it out of the water. Composting, the only option that actually takes place *on* land, as landfill garbage is under it, is hands-down the best choice to protect the stuff we drink, breathe, and live upon.

The battle to responsibly deal with food waste, you see, will be won if by land.

Get the LED Out

It may be time to tell the CFL to get the LED out. No, the Canadian Football League doesn't need to shape up, but there are some compelling reasons to switch from compact fluorescent lighting (CFL) to bulbs that use light-emitting diodes (LED).

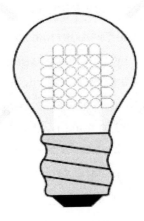

A diode is an essential component of all electronics, ensuring electricity flows only in the direction you want it to. The batteries integral to my home's solar-electric system would leak their sun-generated energy back to the solar panels at night if not for diodes. Invented near the turn of the last century, the tiny semiconductor diodes of today evolved from mammoth vacuum-tube affairs found in the guts of 1950s-era radios and TVs.

Once found mainly in calculator and clock displays, advances over the past two decades have made LEDs practical for home and workplace lighting. Two of their more appealing qualities are that they use very little electricity, and they last, well, almost forever.

When compact fluorescent (CFL) lights came into commercial production in the 1980s they were touted as more ecologically friendly than incandescent lights. Compared to incandescent bulbs, which haven't changed much since Thomas Edison's time, CFLs use far less energy, about one-fourth as much. And they last longer, up to 8,000 hrs. Under ideal conditions (more on that later), the old kind have a 1,200-hour lifespan. Plus, CFLs are so darn cute, all curled up like that.

However, the CFL bulb has a dirty little secret: In its ballast, the sealed, heavy section between the curlicue bulb and the threads, is mercury, a potent neurotoxin. It's the stuff that made the Mad Hatter go mad—many 19th century hatters were poisoned by mercury used in making those iconic black beaver-fur hats. A CFL bulb harbors between one and five milligrams of mercury. This is about 500 times the safe ingestion limit set by the US EPA, so if you were planning on eating a CFL bulb, please reconsider.

CFL bulbs are fussy, too. They don't like to be turned on and off a lot, which drastically shortens their life. Humidly irks them as well, leading to an early demise. They're a little slow to "wake up," and they don't like to work when the temperature is below zero, but I can totally sympathize with that.

It's true LED bulbs cost significantly more, but they use one-tenth the electricity of an incandescent bulb of the same brightness. LEDs contain no mercury or other known toxins, and they last a super-long time, at minimum five times longer than CFLs and fifty times longer than incandescents.

Ever break a glass light bulb? It doesn't take much. But LEDs are nearly indestructible. Plus, they don't care how many times they're switched on and off in a day, and will work in extreme cold or hot environments.

Pretend for a minute you don't care about power consumption or toxic metals. And if you don't have to pretend, please keep that to yourself. According to Colorado-based Intermountain Rural Electric Association, a home with 24 LED bulbs would spend, including bulb purchase, $2,160.00 on lighting over the life of an average LED bulb, assuming $0.12 per KW-hr. Using incandescents of equivalent size, though, would cost $11,424.00, over five times as much.

Whether you're a tree hugger or not, the math works just the same. Using LED lighting adds up pretty nicely.

Alternative Gardening

Here's a recipe for gardening success: Well-drained loam. Adequate nitrogen. Plenty of organic matter. Good soil porosity. Yep—just the ticket to remediate an oil spill.

Although bulk-storage facilities, tanker semi-trucks and train cars are occasionally the source of petroleum spills, it's surprising how often a faulty home-heating oil tank or even a leaky auto gas tank can lead to significant soil and water contamination.

When three-fourths of "soil" is "oil" you may wonder why cleaning up oil even matters. More than once I've heard grumblings to the effect that oil is a natural product that comes out of the ground, so it may as well go right back in.

Granted there's logic to that, but with precious few exceptions, oil is found deep in the ground—essentially the other end of the earth from where we live—in zones far removed from drinking water aquifers. I'm not a livestock expert, but I'm pretty sure "horse apples" originate at one

specific end of a horse, and while they're all natural, shouldn't go in the other end. A coarse analogy, but a fair one. Oil is OK *under* the ground; not so much *on* the ground.

Dealing with contaminated water takes a lot of electricity, engineers and consultants, plus an obscene amount of money. So it's important to deal with oil-soaked dirt—which can be remediated by gardening—before rain leaches dissolved-phase petroleum into groundwater.

I can hear some collective head-scratching out there, or maybe that's the sound of everyone closing this book, so I'll clarify that oil does dissolve in water. It happens to a small degree, in the parts-per-million range, but it's more than enough to make your coffee taste and smell like high-test gas.

In the aftermath of a big spill, petroleum-laced soil can be trucked to an incinerator or hazardous-waste landfill. These are costly options, but sometimes there is little choice. For the homeowner or farmer with a modest-size spill, though, it's possible to "garden" the oil away.

Soil microbes drive this "gardening" process, also called bioremediation. While some oil vaporizes, the vast majority is broken down by native bacteria and fungi already present in the soil. They adapt to "run on oil," eating hydrocarbons and leaving only carbon dioxide and water. While special lab-developed microbes are for sale, native ones do just as well, often better, and are free.

Oxygen is also critical. Oil breaks down at an infinitesimally slow pace in anaerobic, or oxygen-free, conditions. On the other hand, well-managed "gardens" of contaminated soil can be clean in one or two years.

Organic matter greatly increases the surface area that microbes can colonize, and helps with porosity to allow oxygen in. Finally, a little nitrogen at the beginning of the process gives the microbes a boost to get going.

Because of leaching potential, 8"-10" of affected soil is spread on a foot of clean sand over heavy plastic such as bunker-silo covering. The edges should be bermed to prevent runoff. Amendments such as compost and manure are worked in, and the oil garden is rototilled several times per season. Lab analysis, or in some cases field instruments, mark progress until petroleum is no longer detected. Then the soil can be used for any purpose so long as it stays on the owner's property.

Sowing cover crops like buckwheat can expedite the whole affair. Fungi typically colonize root systems, thus increasing surface area for bacteria to live. Studies show plants will not take up petroleum the way they do heavy metals, which is good news for anything feeding on vegetation grown in an "oil garden."

Bioremediation is encouraged by State and local regulators in many instances, and they can often help monitor these "gardens" for you and offer advice on tending them.

Water Wellness 101

Water testing is kind of like academic or medical testing. The Algebra exam tells how you're faring in that subject but not in English, and your foot x-ray won't reveal how your eyes are doing. Similarly, a coliform test can  determine if your well is being impacted by your septic or by manure runoff, but it won't tell you if residues from a chemical spill are getting in your water. Those two things require different tests, and possibly even different labs.

The best time to test a well for anything is in late spring/ early summer when the water table is highest. For each kind of test, the lab will provide the correct type and size of sample bottle along with instructions for taking the sample, and will help you interpret test results.

218

While no well is pollution-proof, a dug well is more at risk for contamination from surface runoff. A drilled well is more secure, but no matter how deep it is, it's still vulnerable to surface contamination near the wellhead. No drilled well is ever in solid rock. Good thing, too, because that would only result in a dry hole in the ground. Water flows into a borehole at various depths through bedding planes (in the case of sedimentary rock), joints and fissures. Contaminants can sometimes be drawn into a well along those same channels.

Broadly speaking, there are three categories of water quality measurements: Biological, inorganic, and organic. In terms of biological, the most common indicator of potential disease pathogens in the water is the presence of coliform bacteria. Some coliforms are harmless and occur naturally in soil, but fecal coliforms live exclusively in the digestive tract of warm-blooded animals. The presence of fecal coliform bacteria could indicate pollution from a septic system or from animal manure. It's a good idea to do an annual total coliform test on your well water, which has a minimal cost. Should you need to disinfect your well, the NYS Department of Health can give you instructions for doing so.

Contaminants such as nitrate, lead, arsenic, cadmium, chromium, copper and cobalt are considered inorganic. Nitrates from agricultural fertilizer and/ or manure application can sicken or even kill infants. And although adults aren't affected, a high nitrate level indicates that pesticides may also be getting into the water. Many older pesticides contained high levels of lead, arsenic and copper. These heavy metals do not break down, and some farms still have high levels of these metals in the soil. Cadmium and chromium are released from smelting operations, and also when colored paper is burned. These elements can leach into the groundwater.

Water hardness from calcium and magnesium, as well as iron, chloride and sulfur, are inorganics which can leave deposits or stains, and may cause objectionable smells or tastes. At very high levels, some of these elements are toxic. Prices for tests vary, but checking for inorganics is very affordable.

"Organic" is a misleading term, because while eating organic food is good, consuming organic chemicals is definitely not. Pesticides, degreasers, gas, oil, antifreeze, and many paints are all organic chemicals. How do organic pollutants get into our water? It's shockingly easy to pollute groundwater here in the Northeast where it rains a lot and the distance to groundwater is relatively short. Leaky tanks, fuel overfills, floor drains, and even surface spills can contaminate a well.

The old saying that oil and water don't mix is a partial truth. The real story is that, in scientific terminology, they blend a teensy little bit, which is more than enough to pollute water. Benzene, a constituent of gas and diesel, is 0.018% soluble in water. Given that the allowable limit of benzene in drinking water is 0.07 parts per billion (ppb), the concentration of benzene near a gas spill could be something like 180,000 ppb. Fortunately, the odor threshold for benzene is 50-100 ppb, so you would not unknowingly drink benzene at such high levels. Unless maybe you had the worst head cold ever.

It's not uncommon for chemicals like paint thinner or degreasers that get washed down the drain at home to enter groundwater through septic leach fields or weep tanks and find their way into drinking water wells. Unlike benzene, most solvents have high odor thresholds, meaning one could ingest fairly significant levels without realizing it. A fuel oil spill in your garden could disappear in one season if you added manure and rototilled often, but under the ground, organic chemicals break down very slowly, taking decades, if not centuries.

Because groundwater is not static but is always (slowly, in general) flowing, contamination from previous incidents can suddenly show up years later. A corollary to that is the fact that contamination from one property can, and will, migrate underground much the way smoke from your chimney wafts on the breeze instead of halting at your property line. It is in fact everyone's business when chemicals are spilled on private land.

Testing for organics is complicated: for example, checking for gasoline, solvents and other volatiles, or pesticides, or antifreeze all require different tests. It's also more expensive. A lab test for volatiles costs more than one for metals, but far less than for pesticides.

Most contaminants can be removed with the right kind of filtration system, but these can easily cost hundreds of dollars per month to maintain. Occasionally, drilling a new well upgradient from the contaminated area is more cost-effective, and safer, than continued filtration.

The take-home message is that anything that goes onto the ground or down the drain has the potential to get into the drinking water. Let's work together to keep our well water—and our neighbor's water—well.

Chapter Eight

Nature Takes a Few Holidays

WIth Nature's superlative wacky sense of humor, it is kind of embarrassing to write anything for April Fools' Day. But I could not help myself.

Chemical Alert

Health authorities would like to inform residents of the widespread presence of a substance in the local environment known to the International Union of Pure and Applied Chemists (IUPAC) as dihydrogen oxide (DHO).

This unique substance can appear in gaseous, liquid or solid form. Dihydrogen oxide's gaseous phase is colorless and odorless, making it nearly impossible to detect. One of DHO's unusual features is that it can transition directly from a solid to a gas. Its liquid and solid forms are clear and colorless.

Although at this time there's no conclusive evidence that its gaseous form causes health problems, its other phases are known to pose real risks. Contact with the solid form of DHO will cause discomfort, followed by numbness, and in the case of prolonged contact, permanent tissue damage has been documented.

223

The public is also advised to use caution in the proximity of dihydrogen oxide's liquid form, as this compound is able to dissolve a great many substances with which it comes in contact. Most inorganic mineral compounds, as well as some organic chemicals, readily dissolve in dihydrogen oxide. DHO is even able to destroy stone and concrete. In some cases, great quantities have been dissolved.

Dihydrogen oxide is known to damage other materials, and is particularly destructive to wood, paper and ferrous metals. Small to moderate quantities of DHO promote the decay of wood, leather and other organic matter.

Although DHO is a fairly simple molecule, consisting of two hydrogen atoms fused to an oxygen atom, do not underestimate its power. Please use caution in the presence of DHO. In some regions it is known by colloquial, non-IUPAC names such as "agua," "eau," "H-2-O," or "water."

Rare Species

Hikers, anglers and other outdoor enthusiasts are urged to keep an eye out this spring for an elusive plant that may be making a comeback. The so-called stinging rejoinder, *Aculeatus depulsio*, although it is a distant cousin of stinging nettle, *Urtica dioica*, does not actually sting or cause a rash. It is an inconspicuous, native medicinal plant which was over-harvested in the 19th and early 20th centuries, and has been hard to find since that time. However, there is indirect evidence its population could be on the rise.

Its common name comes from the way *Aculeatus depulsio* works on the nervous system. When taken internally, the stinging rejoinder seems to temporarily inhibit neuronal reuptake of glutamate, an excitatory neurotransmitter, in the frontal cortex. In plain English, it makes you smarter for a short time, which explains its popularity. It does lose potency quickly, though, and must be used fresh.

Because it disappeared before the advent of pharmaceutical giants, its active constituents were never isolated or identified. Had they been, you can bet your wallet they would be patent-protected and would cost a fortune today. As with all herbal remedies, be sure to consult your health care provider before using, because they can aggravate certain conditions or interact with medication.

Unfortunately, *Aculeatus depulsio* looks similar to a lot of other plants, and over the years many people who thought they had found a good stinging rejoinder were disappointed when they tried it but it had no effect. *Aculeatus depulsio* leaves are slick-looking, glossy and inviting, but dark; almost always pointed, and occasionally barbed. Its stem has formidable-looking thorns, which often turn out to be harmless. It can reach anywhere from a few inches tall to about six feet, but inevitably winds up being much smaller up close than it looked from a distance. The plant is found in wet, unstable ground, and there exist scads of old anecdotes about people sinking deeper and deeper in mire searching for one.

Aculeatus depulsio was traditionally used to enhance cognition during arguments, especially those in the context of committed relationships, by one or both parties. It was considered unfair to use preemptively, though this cultural norm was sometimes ignored. Especially in cases where one party had betrayed the trust of the other or been needlessly harsh, the injured party might seek out *Aculeatus depulsio* to make a particularly salient rebuke.

Occasionally this would work to devastating effect, but more often than not it would end up being a waste of time. Statistically speaking, most arguments occur at night. But for some reason, the stinging rejoinder is more easily located the following morning, when it may no longer be useful or even desired.

Botanists speculate that *Aculeatus depulsio* numbers may be up, pointing to recent studies which show snappy retorts are on the rise. Sociologists, on the other hand, point out this is only the situation with the younger demographic, and they maintain that social media and "argument Apps" on mobile devices are behind this new trend. Only time will tell.

In the meanwhile, please be on the watch for stinging rejoinders when you're in the great outdoors this spring. Documents dating back to the late 1800s indicate the best day to seek out the rare *Aculeatus depulsio* is the first day of the fourth month.

Biotech Firm Gets GMO Patent

A northern NY biotechnology startup has been granted provisional approval for a patent to genetically modify *Escherichia coli* bacteria for the manufacture of medical-grade compounds. Cell Signals, LLC, based in Depeyster, NY, plans to break ground on an addition to its facility in the spring of 2021. The new research and manufacturing wing, which will more than triple its production capacity, is to be equipped with a state-of-the-art research lab as well as a two-story heated warehouse space with batch-process reactor vats. It is anticipated that as many as six full-time jobs will be added.

The first modification of *E. coli* was done by Dr. Herbert Boyer at a University of California lab in 1978 to make synthetic human insulin, a process that was approved by the U.S. Food and Drug Administration in 1982. Since then, it has become common to modify *E. coli* and other organisms to make life-saving drugs like interferon, a treatment for multiple sclerosis and leukemia. Human growth hormone, Hepatitis C vaccine, and other medicines are also mass-produced in this way.

For the past five years, Cell Signals has been using modified *E. coli* to make ascorbic acid (vitamin C) and acetic acid (vinegar) for food-service and industrial applications. When its new equipment comes online, however, it will be able to create a broad spectrum of chemicals for the pharmaceutical industry on a highly flexible, as-needed basis. While this is seen as a positive development by many, it has generated some criticism.

Perhaps the most controversial product on its patent is a synthetic neuropeptide associated with human bonding and compassion. Related to the hormone oxytocin, this molecule is being called "milk of human kindness," a Shakespearean phrase.

One complaint comes from the dairy industry, which has been lobbying for tough new labeling restrictions on the use of the term "milk." Beverages made from soy, almond, cashew and rice are marketed as milk, a fact which has gotten under the skim of dairy proponents. Should they succeed in regulating what can and cannot be called milk, it is not known how that might affect the sale or use of milk of human kindness.

Not surprisingly, critics of genetically modified (GM) crops and foods are also opposed to the new Cell Signals initiative. To be fair, there is no consensus in the scientific world on the overall health effects of GM products, unlike the case with climate change, where 98 percent of scientists acknowledge both its existence and its genesis. In the lead article in its March 2015 issue, National Geographic concludes with the statement that "The long-term health and ecological consequences [of GM foods] are unknown."

What is startling, though, are harsh words from places which normally champion GM innovations. Responding to a sidebar in *The Wall Street Journal* that mentioned Cell Signals' intentions, a spokesperson from the right-wing think tank The Cato Institute blasted the plan. "We can't have cheap milk of human kindness flooding the market. Compassion is a rare commodity, and we should keep it that way," said Ernest Mendacity, a press liaison. "What if this stuff gets into our food supply? We might have people starting to feel happy who don't deserve it. Happiness should only come from greed. I don't think the FDA has thought this through."

For its part, the U.S. Food and Drug Administration states that "Based on the results of extensive laboratory analysis, we find no statistically significant difference between genetically modified and naturally-sourced milk of human kindness in any of the parameters normally used to characterize that product."

Wishing you a happy April Fools' Day, and an abundance of human kindness.

Climate Change and Animal Population

A week-long climate-change symposium at the University of

Bologna in Italy wrapped up recently, and scientists have reached broad agreement about potential changes in future animal population size and distribution. Although much of the news on the effects of climate change on animals is negative, there seems to be an unexpected bright spot on the horizon.

The current pattern of temperate-zone species like grizzly bears and white-tail deer migrating north into the Arctic is likely to accelerate. At the same time, some polar-region animal populations are in steep decline as a result of reduced snow and ice cover. Arctic caribou, snow leopards and wolverines may be in worse shape than previously thought.

Some of the "animals" that benefit from a changing climate are agricultural pests. Many destructive insects like the brown marmorated stink bug and the coffee berry borer have expanded both in range and population size in the past 25 years. This trend is also expected to accelerate.

However, computer modeling indicates a habitat expansion for at least one large mammal species. The reclusive hominid *Gigantopithecus blacki*, a primate once thought extinct, is better known as Bigfoot, Sasquatch or other names depending on region. While often associated with the Pacific Northwest, a fossil jaw of *Gigantopithecus blacki* was found in southern St. Lawrence County in 1957, indicating it may have lived in NY

229

State's Adirondacks since the last glacial period.

The Bigfoot Field Researchers' Organization, the only scientific research organization investigating this issue, has record of nearly 100 sightings in NY State. Many of these are in northern NY, with documented cases in Hamilton, St. Lawrence, Essex, and Fulton counties. Warren County leads the state with twelve sightings dating back to 1990. The fact that most encounters have been reported since 2000 suggests the trend towards more *Gigantopithecus blacki* is already underway.

Because they're omnivores, *Gigantopithecus blacki* can fill a similar niche as black bears, coyotes and raccoons. Researchers believe that as their range expands, *Gigantopithecus blacki* will help clean up road kills, easing the burden on Public Works crews. It's even possible that a larger "Bigfoot" population could help reduce solid waste at landfills by scavenging food.

Though their relative numbers will rise, *Gigantopithecus blacki* is a species whose total numbers are unlikely to reach levels that would cause conflicts with humans. Wildlife biologists are already gearing up for a *Gigantopithecus blacki* rabies vaccination program.

Because some past "Bigfoot" reports have turned out to be hoaxes, many people still believe that *Gigantopithecus blacki* is the stuff of legend. However, one of the attendees at the recent climate-change symposium in Bologna, Dr. Stanislaus Boguslavski of Paul Smith's College Cryptozoology Department, is working to change public opinion in NY State.

"Basic Algebra can prove climate change and *Gigantopithecus blacki* are both legitimate," Dr. Boguslavski says. "According to our studies, climate change and Bigfoot are controversial topics, which is great because you can set up an equation to factor out the term 'controversial,' thus leaving 'topics' period. End of argument."

I couldn't have put it better myself. Happy April First!

Valentine Trees

It's impossible for a parent to choose a favorite child, or at least that's what I tell my kids—and it's almost as difficult for an arborist to pick a single best-liked tree. For different reasons, I have many pet species. One of the, um, apples of my eye is a species I've never laid eyes on, but it's one I've appreciated since early childhood.

Native to Central America, the cacao tree (*Theobroma cacao* to arborists) grows almost exclusively within twenty degrees latitude either side of the equator—in other words, where most of us ould rather be on February 14. The seeds of the cacao tree have been ground and made into a drink known by its Native American (probably Nahuatl) name, chocolate, for as many as 4,000 years.

The cacao is a small tree, about 15-20 feet tall, bearing

6- to 12-inch long seed pods. Packed around the 30-40 cacao beans in each pod is a sweet gooey pulp, which historically was also consumed. After harvest, cacao beans go through a fermentation process and are then dried and milled into powder.

In pre-contact times, chocolate was a frothy, bitter drink often mixed with chilies and cornmeal. Mayans and Aztecs drank it mainly for its medicinal properties—more on that later. In the late 1500s, a Spanish Jesuit who had been to Mexico described chocolate as being "Loathsome to such as are not acquainted with it, having a scum or froth that is very unpleasant taste." It's understandable, then, that it was initially slow to take off in Europe.

Chocolate became wildly popular, though, after brilliant innovations such as adding sugar and omitting chili peppers. Another reason for its meteoric rise in demand is that it seemed to have pleasant effects. One of these was similar to that of tea or coffee. There isn't much caffeine in chocolate, but it has nearly 400 known constituents, and a number of these compounds are uppers.

Chief among them is theobromine, which has no bromine—go figure. It's a chemical sibling to caffeine, and its name supposedly derives from the Greek for "food of the gods." Even if people knew it more closely translates to "stink of the gods," it's unlikely it would put a damper on chocolate sales.

These days chocolate is recognized as a potent antioxidant, but throughout the ages it's had a reputation for being an aphrodisiac. I assume this explains the tradition of giving chocolate to one's lover on Valentine's Day. Does chocolate live up to its rumored powers? Another stimulant it contains, phenylethylamine (PEA), may account for its repute.

Closely related to amphetamine, PEA facilitates the release of dopamine, the "feel good" chemical in the brain's reward center. Turns out that when you fall in love, your brain is practically dripping with dopamine. Furthermore, at least three compounds in chocolate mimic the effects of marijuana. They bind to the same receptors In our brains as THC, the active ingredient in pot, releasing more dopamine and also serotonin, another brain chemical associated with happiness.

Don't be alarmed at this news; these things are quite minimal compared to what real drugs can do. Consuming chocolate has never impaired my ability to operate heavy machinery (lack of training and experience have, though).

Most people would agree that chocolate is no substitute for love, but these natural chemical effects may be why romance and chocolate are so intertwined. Well, that and marketing.

Dogs can't metabolize theobromine very well, and a modest amount of chocolate, especially dark, can be toxic to them. This is why you shouldn't get your dog a box of chocolates on Valentine's Day, no matter how much you love them. And assuming it's spayed or neutered, your pooch won't benefit from any of chocolate's other potential effects anyway.

Great Pumpkins

Linus, the precocious, blanket-toting character from the "Peanuts" world, waited faithfully for The Great Pumpkin all night on Halloween in spite of being disappointed every year. Perhaps his unwavering belief in the mythical pumpkin was spurred on by the fact that almost every year brings the world a bigger "great pumpkin" of the sort one can measure and—at least potentially—eat.

In fact, pumpkins have gotten so big in recent years that folks have cleaned them out and paddled around in them. Heck, if you are not claustrophobic, maybe you could even live in one. If the Old Lady Who Lived in a Shoe thought it was great to find a rent-free boot, imagine how thrilled she would have been to inhabit a giant pumpkin. But then I suppose the kids would have eaten her out of house and home.

Over the past three decades, giant pumpkin enthusiasts (that's regular-size people; giant produce) have developed varieties that attain jaw-dropping proportions. And they (the produce, primarily) are getting bigger faster. In 1979 the world record was 198 kg, which jumped to over 453 kg in in 1996, and to a 1,190 kg monster Atlantic pumpkin raised by Belgian farmer Mathias Willemijns in 2016. Now that would be a dream come true for Linus.

Growing big pumpkins begins with the right genetics, and you can bet that the seeds from these record-holders will fetch a good price. Beyond that it is a lot of daily attention, especially later in the season when the developing pumpkins need copious amounts of water. These growers put in a lot of hours in their attempts at agricultural overachievement.

Being the scholarly lad he was, Linus probably knew that

pumpkins are actually a type of winter squash, one of many varieties first selected for and cultivated by First Nations. Squash, in fact, is an Algonquin word adopted by Europeans. We chose the Greek-based "pumpkin" to describe the ribbed orange variety, mostly because "The Great Squash" didn't have the right ring to it.

Hubbard and butternut squash, and the small hard pie pumpkins we grow today are among the many squash types that the Haudenosaunee, or Iroquois, were raising on the shores of Lakes Erie and Ontario at the time of European contact. From ancient times until today (or maybe tomorrow if they are busy at the moment), Haudenosaunee farmers have dried strips of pumpkin and squash for use in late winter after the storage life of most squashes has run its course. If old-time longhouses had dehumidifiers and thermostats, those pumpkins and squash could have lasted all winter.

Successful storage actually begins in the field or garden. Pumpkins and squash will last longer if you bring them in before the first hard frost (below -1 Celsius). Always support the bottom when picking them up, and never carry them by the stem; if that breaks, rot will set in. For pumpkins, a 10-day hardening-off treatment of 26-29 C at 80% humidity will help harden the rind and prolong storage life. This treatment isn't necessary for butternut, turban and Hubbard, and will actually harm acorn squash.

In terms of storage conditions, the critical thresholds are 10 and 70. Never cooler than 10 C, or more humid than 70%. The ideal numbers are 15 degrees and 60% humidity. Store pumpkins and squash away from apples, which produce ethylene gas that will hasten ripening, and shorten storage life. Check stored squash every few weeks, as one rotten one can spread decay to others.

Under good conditions, acorn squash will store for 5-8 weeks. Pie pumpkins, as well as buttercup squash, often make it through the winter, and it's not unheard of for a Hubbard or butternut to last into the following summer. Because the record-breaking pumpkins of today have Hubbard genetics, I'd expect those leviathans might last a good while. But no one is likely to build a storage room around a one-ton pumpkin.

It would seem this agricultural super-sizing may have been predicted fifty-odd years ago by little Linus. Maybe I should revisit those old comics to read what else the child philosopher had to say.

Thanks for Giving

If the Pilgrims had known what a big deal Thanksgiving was going to become in America they would undoubtedly have taken some pictures. Even the menu has been lost to us,  although Wampanoag oral history, plus a few Pilgrim grocery receipts found by archeologists, suggest there was corn, beans and squash as well as fowl and venison. Beyond that there may have been chestnuts, sun chokes ("Jerusalem" artichokes), cranberries and a variety of seafood.

Many historians believe the Pilgrims would have all perished during the winter of 1620 if not for food provided by the Wampanoags, whose land they appropriated. In the spring of 1621, some Wampanoags gave the Pilgrims crop seeds, as well as a tutorial—possibly an App; we can't be sure—on the production, storage and preservation of food crops including corn, beans, and squash.

We're not even certain if it was October or November, but that fall the Pilgrims gave thanks for Native American agriculture, and feasted upon its bounty for three days straight. The Wampanoags probably gave thanks that there weren't more ships full of Pilgrims on the horizon just then.

Barley was the only European-sourced crop that the Pilgrims managed to raise in 1621. Unfortunately, they seemed unaware it could be eaten. Fortunately, there was plenty of beer at the first Thanksgiving.

While corn, beans and squash, "The Three Sisters," were and still are grown by many native peoples in the Americas, other indigenous crops will grace American Thanksgiving tables each year. Maybe you'll have appetizers like mixed nuts before dinner. Peanuts are a big-time Native American crop. Pecans and sunflower seeds, too. And everyone likes corn chips with dip. Those hot and sweet peppers and tomatoes in the salsa are Native American foods. Prefer dip made with avocado? Yep, another native food. And the same for popcorn.

Turkeys are indigenous to the New World, but so are a lot of the fixings. Pass the (New World) cranberry sauce, please. It wouldn't be Thanksgiving without mashed potatoes to soak up the gravy. White or "Irish" potatoes are a New World crop, as are sweet potatoes. We can thank Native American agronomists for green and Lima beans. Don't forget the squash—Native peoples developed many varieties, including Hubbard and butternut squash, and pumpkins, which are technically a winter squash.

Which brings us to the iconic Thanksgiving pumpkin pie—I think just about everyone is thankful for that treat. Nothing goes with pie like ice cream, which is not from the New World, but some great flavorings are. Maple-walnut is one of the earliest ice cream varieties in New England, two indigenous flavors that go together famously. While not from the Northeast, vanilla is from the Americas, and so is chocolate. If you add some toppings like strawberry or blueberry, or even pineapple, sauce, you'll be having more Native American foods for dessert.

Wishing you all a happy and healthy Thanksgiving, filled with family and gratitude. Among other things, we can be grateful to Native peoples and their crops. But please, don't blame them if you have to loosen your belt a notch or two afterward.

Pining for That Evergreen Smell

Of all the memorable aromas of the winter holiday season, nothing evokes its spirit quite like the smell of fresh-cut evergreen. Although over 80% of American households where Christmas is observed use artificial trees, about eleven million families still bring home a real tree.

Every species of conifer has its own mixture of sweet-smelling terpenols and esters that account for their "piney woods" perfume. Some people prefer the fragrance of a particular tree, possibly one they had as a child. A natural Christmas tree is, among other things, a giant holiday potpourri. No chemistry lab can make a polyvinylchloride tree smell like fresh pine, fir or spruce.

The origins of the Christmas tree are unclear, but evergreen trees, wreaths, and boughs were used by a number of ancient peoples, including the Egyptians, to symbolize eternal life. In sixteenth-century Germany, Martin Luther apparently helped kindle (so to speak) the custom of the indoor home Christmas tree by bringing an evergreen into his house and decorating it with candles. For centuries, Christmas trees were brought into homes on December 24th and were not removed until after the Christian feast of Epiphany on January 6th.

In terms of favorites, the firs—Douglas, balsam, and Fraser—are very popular aromatic evergreens. Grand and concolor fir smell great too. When kept in water, firs all have excellent needle retention.

Scots and white pine also keep their needles well. While our native white pine is more fragrant than Scots, the latter far outsells the former, possibly because the sturdy Scots can bear quite a load of decorations without its branches drooping.

Not only do spruces have strong branches, they tend to have a strongly pyramidal shape. Spruces are not quite as fragrant as firs or pines, though, but they're great options for those who like short-needle trees. Many field guides say white spruce buds smell like cat urine, but based on robust white spruce sales, plenty of folks don't think so.

Do yourself and the local economy a favor this year by purchasing a natural tree from a local vendor, who can help you select the best kind to suit your needs, and also let you know how fresh they are. Some trees at large retail outlets were cut many weeks before they show up at stores. Of course, cutting your own tree from a Christmas tree grower ensures freshness and can be a memorable family experience.

For the best fragrance and needle retention, cut a one- to two-inch "cookie" from the base before placing your tree in the stand, and fill the reservoir every two days. Research indicates products claiming to extend needle life don't work, so save your money. Tree lights with LED bulbs don't dry out the needles as the old style did. Your tree will last longer, and so will your electric bill.

Whatever your traditions, may your family, friends, and evergreens all be well-hydrated, sweet-scented and a source of good cheer this holiday season.

Yule Logs

The tradition of burning a Yule or Christmas log has largely fizzled out in most parts of the world. Although often depicted as a

modest-size birch log, the monster Yule logs back in 6th and 7th century Germany were tree trunks that were intended to burn all day, in some cultures for twelve days, without being entirely consumed. It was important that an unburned portion of the log remain after the marathon Yule-burn, because this insured good luck in the upcoming year. The Yule remnant was tucked away in a safe place in the home, presumably after it was extinguished, and was used to light the following year's Yule log.

While a birch log is picturesque, it doesn't compare with many

240

other hardwoods in terms of heat value and how long it will burn. All people are created with equal value; with logs, not so much.

Heat value, whether from coal, oil or wood, is measured in BTUs, or British thermal units. One BTU represents the energy required to heat a pound of water one degree Fahrenheit. If this sounds awkward, consider the more recent chimera, the Celsius heat unit (Chu), the energy needed to heat a *pound* of water one degree celsius. Brilliant.

Most people in this part of the country know that fuel wood is usually some type of hardwood, a misnomer term. Certain hardwoods, shorthand for deciduous trees, are actually softer than softwoods, or conifers. Basswood and eastern cottonwood, for example, have a BTU rating per dry cord of around 12 million, lower than that of white pine (16 million) and balsam (20 million).

As those who heat with wood know, hickory, hard maple, and black locust are tops for firewood, producing almost 30 million BTUs (mBTU) per cord. You'd have to burn twice as much butternut or aspen to get the same amount of heat! Beech, white oak and ironwood (hop hornbeam) rate quite high, around 25 mBTU/ cord. The photogenic paper birch has about 20, respectable but not a premium fuel.

I should say here that firewood BTU charts from various reputable sources differ, at times significantly, in reported values. As in all such cases where authorities disagree, one could conveniently choose the value most convenient to one's purpose. Not that I would ever do that.

Of course there are considerations aside from BTU value in

choosing firewood. Even though balsam heats better than butternut, it throws a lot of sparks as it burns, creating a potential hazard in an open-hearth fireplace. Moisture is also critical. Well, critical not to have it. When wet wood is burned, much of the wood's heat value goes into boiling off the water. Fresh-cut elm is 70 percent water by weight—you'd get very little heat from that, assuming you could even keep it lit.

Outdoor furnaces, because they have a blower, are capable of burning green wood. This might seem convenient, but to burn unseasoned wood like that you'd spend twice as much time and lift twice the amount of wood compared to dry fuel.

In the Balkans and parts of southern Europe, the genuine Yule-log tradition still burns on, while in Quebec and some other regions as well, a much tastier Yule log is popular. But the Yule cake or bûche de Noël, a time-honored Christmas dessert, is not burned. At least not on purpose.

If you're one of the few families who will burn an actual Yule log in an open hearth this year, you probably have a good chunk of dry hard maple or hickory set aside, plus a remnant of last year's log with which to light it. But if that's not your tradition, you can join millions who tune in to the televised Yule Log programs this holiday season. While there are many from which to choose these days, the first one has been going since its first U.S. appearance way back in 1967.

Considering that the original TV Yule log was lit fifty years ago and has not burned out yet, we could probably solve the world's energy problems if we could determine what species of wood was used, and plant just a few acres of those trees. But the U.S. Department of Energy was doing a lot of secret research in the 1960s, so it may be classified. Maybe this will spark a new batch of conspiracy hypotheses as to why we have been kept in the dark about this new super-Yule wood.

Chapter Nine

Around Again

When it comes to personal growth, the Wicked Witch of the West had the right idea. Quite possibly she got it from monarch butterflies, which must exist in Oz, since they are found worldwide except for polar regions. Many times, a rearrangement of the self-image we have come to know is needed to achieve our fullest potential. In my experience this is always hard, and seldom voluntary.

Self-Help and Soup

We commonly refer to difficult times, periods of grief or anguish, in terms of dissolution. A person might go to pieces, fall apart, dissolve in tears, or have a meltdown. This latter can describe anything from a childhood tantrum to a coworker who loses composure due to stress. Meltdowns are short-lived.

Breakdowns last longer—weeks, months, even years. People in this state are generally unable to function well, if at all, in jobs or relationships. Nearly all who have breakdowns recover, and afterward it is not unusual for them to be different. They may have a new perspective, or choose a trajectory more in line with their dreams. Oftentimes as a result of surviving a very dark period, an individual will shape their life to better suit them, and report being happier than before.

In order to make the dramatic leap from glorified maggot to graceful flying machine, a caterpillar has a complete breakdown, during which it melts down. A caterpillar is of course the juvenile stage of a moth or butterfly, and most are stubby, cigar-shaped, soft-bodied crawly things that somehow become gossamer-winged wonders. We know they enter a pupal phase to switch costumes, but until fairly recently we knew more about what went on inside Clark Kent's phone booth than what happened during pupation. Thanks to electron micrography and other fancy stuff, we now know a tiny bit more.

Some caterpillars produce silk to weave cocoons in which to pupate. Others, for example the monarch, make a chrysalis, a pupal case with a membranous skin around it. Once housing is settled, the hard part begins. Take the monarch again. Ensconced in its regal,  gold-flecked chrysalis, the cute, stripey chub of a caterpillar releases enzymes which dissolve its body. All of it. For a time, that elegant chrysalis is full of nothing but green caterpillar soup. Now that's a meltdown.

As the caterpillar liquifies, most of its cells burst open. This is akin to hammering to dust a Lego car to make a house rather than re-purposing the same blocks. There are a few cells, though, which make it through the blender. These are akin to stem cells, and biologists have dubbed them "imaginal cells." This is wonderfully poetic, as if part of the caterpillar could always imagine flying.

I had heard that a caterpillar's immune system perceived

imaginal cells as foreign material, and would try to eliminate them. This makes for an even stronger metaphor, because we all resist change at first, but alas, science does not confirm this immune-response idea.

In a sense, imaginal cells do foresee the future winged adult, as they contain its DNA, the butterfly blueprint. As far as I can tell, no one knows quite how imaginal cells take that Lego-dust and fashion new kinds of tissue from them. It's better than magic. There are a few other items in caterpillar soup. From the time it hatches, a larva has within it a fixed number of somewhat flat, more-or-less round structures of highly organized imaginal cells called imaginal discs. Each disc telescopes out like, I don't know, a telescope maybe, to become an appendage such as a wing or leg.

By the time the pupal chamber unzips and an adult monarch emerges from its chrysalis to rub its bleary eyes, not a drop of caterpillar soup remains. All of it was supped up to serve its new life as a butterfly. If said butterfly belongs to the fourth and last generation of the summer, it might want a cup of coffee before its 3,000-mile trip south. In spring, monarchs take three generations, relay-style, to get all the way north, but the final brood flies to Mexico for the winter in one marathon shot.

Thinking about chrysali is always timely, as any season is a good one to reflect and imagine. And to enjoy some soup while pondering meltdowns and transformations.

Cultivating Philosophy

It occurs to me that having more second-rate gardeners in the world could help make it a better place.

Recently I stumbled upon a cache of flower seeds I had been looking for all spring. Like a squirrel which does not remember all the spots it stashed nuts the previous fall, I can't seem to keep track of my things either.

The seeds in question are a pole bean called 'Scarlet Runner,' a variety grown primarily for their brilliant red flowers that bloom all season long, and not so much for food. On a trellis it makes a spectacular privacy screen; on a tripod of poles in the center of the garden it is a stunning eye-catcher. Bird lovers appreciate it because is a favorite of hummingbirds. It's really quite an enchanting legume.

I was pleased to be reunited with my prodigal bean seeds, but all the prime garden spaces were filled. Plus, it was kind of late in the season to plant scarlet runners; normally they would be ready to bloom by then. And at that moment I was on a tight schedule and dead-tired besides. There were so many reasons to just put them away for next spring.

But then I thought about the weed-choked berm of bank-run gravel I had piled against the porch foundation a few years ago to try and keep the concrete from buckling any further. The location was sunny, but the soil, if you could call it that, was poor, and it dried out fast. In the ten minutes I had to spare, I tore out a patch of weeds, gouged a trench in the gravel, scattered the seeds along the trench, threw the remains of a bag of potting mix over them, and splashed a bucket of water onto the lot.

In an ideal world I would have set up a trellis beforehand. Then removed a quantity of gravel and replaced it with topsoil. And made a straight-edge out of some twine strung between two stakes in order to have a perfectly straight row. But we know all too well this is not an ideal world. We don't always have the luxury of planning ahead.

I took the actions I did with the resources available at the time, knowing it honestly might come to nothing. But there was a chance, if the seeds were viable and it rained enough, that there might be a fabulous wall of scarlet flowers late that summer. Such probability would have been zero if I had not done an imperfect job of sowing seeds in a questionable location.

That is when the metaphor hit me—which thankfully did not hurt very much—that shoddy gardening is exactly what we need right now. Not bad soil and crooked lines of plants. But if we were to take every possible occasion to drop a latent germ of kindness, even in unlikely places, no matter how harried we are, it could yield something beautiful.

It might not, of course. But it certainly won't unless we take risks. Every day brings us loads of opportunities to plant such seeds, and rarely is it under the best of conditions. They seem to usually happen when we are tired, and out of our comfort zone—in the

249

lousy soil and tall weeds, so to speak—as well.

Sadly, I generally notice these times after I have failed to act on them. But not always. I think it gets better with practice. Maybe we could put aside our busy-ness for a minute if we were to get the sense our coworker needed more than just a passing "Hi, how's it going?" Perhaps we could refrain from reacting the next time someone is rude on the phone or in traffic, and instead offer them a good thought.

It could be the person who was a jerk to us is a hair's breadth from some act of desperation or violence, and one kind thought or gesture, one fewer negative reaction—is what turns the tide. Unlike my scarlet runners in the gravel pile, though, we will never be able to check on the outcome of the humble seeds we scatter.

What matters is that we offer our dusty little kindness, even if it is merely a good thought, to whatever soil is available. Nothing may come of it. But it could be transformative, depending how much sun and rain turn up once we depart the scene. If we risk taking a moment to be present and plant a seed in less-than-ideal conditions, the chances of a flower blooming there later may be small. No one knows. But what is for sure is that if we do nothing, the chances are nil.

By the way, those scarlet runners turned out fabulous.

CPSIA information can be obtained
at www.ICGtesting.com
Printed in the USA
BVHW041925051218
534867BV00017B/230/P